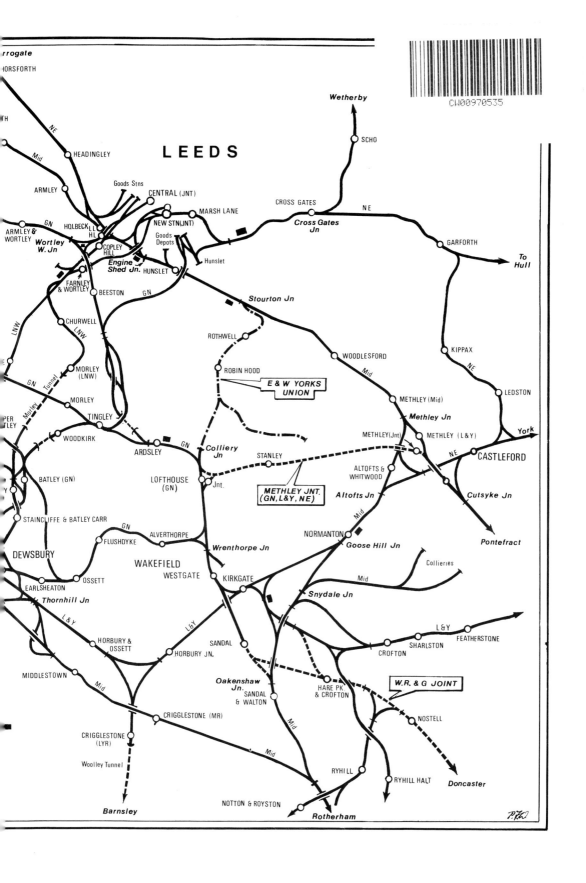

rrogate

HORSFORTH

TH

NE

Mid

HEADINGLEY

LEEDS

ARMLEY

Goods Stns

CENTRAL (JNT)

MARSH LANE

CROSS GATES

NE

GN

Cross Gates Jn

NEW STN(JNT)

GARFORTH

ARMLEY & WORTLEY

HOLBECK LL HL

Wortley W. Jn

COPLEY HILL

Goods Depots

To Hull

Engine Shed Jn.

HUNSLET

Hunslet

FARNLEY & WORTLEY

BEESTON

GN

Stourton Jn

LNW

CHURWELL

LNW

ROTHWELL

WOODLESFORD

KIPPAX

Mid

NE

MORLEY (LNW)

ROBIN HOOD

E & W YORKS UNION

METHLEY (Mid)

LEDSTON

GN

Morley Tunnel

MORLEY

PER TLEY

TINGLEY

Methley Jn

York

WOODKIRK

GN

Colliery Jn

METHLEY(Jnt)

METHLEY (L&Y)

CASTLEFORD

ARDSLEY

STANLEY

ALTOFTS & WHITWOOD

NE

BATLEY (GN)

LOFTHOUSE (GN)

Jnt.

METHLEY JNT. (GN,L&Y, NE)

Altofts Jn

Cutsyke Jn

STAINCLIFFE & BATLEY CARR

GN

ALVERTHORPE

NORMANTON

Mid

Pontefract

DEWSBURY

FLUSHDYKE

Wrenthorpe Jn

Goose Hill Jn

Collieries

WAKEFIELD

WESTGATE

KIRKGATE

Mid

EARLSHEATON

OSSETT

Snydale Jn

L&Y

Thornhill Jn

L&Y

L&Y

SHARLSTON

FEATHERSTONE

HORBURY & OSSETT

SANDAL

CROFTON

MIDDLESTOWN

HORBURY JN.

Mid

Oakenshaw Jn.

SANDAL & WALTON

HARE PK & CROFTON

W.R. & G JOINT

CRIGGLESTONE (MR)

Mid

NOSTELL

CRIGGLESTONE (LYR)

Mid

Woolley Tunnel

RYHILL

RYHILL HALT

Doncaster

Barnsley

NOTTON & ROYSTON

Rotherham

Wetherby

SCHO

P.Kd

RAIL CENTRES:
LEEDS/BRADFORD

RAIL CENTRES:
LEEDS/BRADFORD

STEPHEN R. BATTY

Nottingham
Booklaw Publications

First published 1989
by Ian Allan Ltd

©Ian Allan Ltd 1989

This edition published 2005 by Booklaw Publications
382, Carlton Hill, Nottingham NG4 1JA

ISBN 1-901945-22-7

Printed by
The Amadeus Press, Cleckheaton, West Yorkshire

Title page, left:
**Class '5' 4-6-0 No 44826 clears Wortley West
Junction with the 09.25 King's Cross-Bradford
train on 29 April 1967.** *M. Dunnett*

Title page, right:
**LYR Class 'A' 0-6-0 No 1293 at Mirfield shed. The
small 'L&Y' lettering on the tender is unusual.**
LYRS

This page:
**Class 45 'Peak' 1Co-Co1 No 45020 growls out of
Leeds City on a bright 20 September 1975 with the
17.38 Leeds-Bristol.** *Brian Morrison*

Contents

Introduction

Barely 10 miles separate the centres of Leeds and Bradford, but it would be impossible to find two other cities in the United Kingdom which are so close together and yet, topographically and industrially speaking, so far apart. Bradford is almost surrounded by steep, high hills, but Leeds is readily accessible from all directions. Water transport in Bradford was limited to a connection into the Leeds & Liverpool Canal at Shipley, whereas Leeds straddled the River Aire and had access to canals which operated to all four points of the compass. The wool trade was originally common to both places, but during the 19th century Bradford's mills came to dominate the nation's woollen industry whilst Leeds reduced its dependence and diversified into tailoring and heavy engineering.

Railway development in the two cities was similarly marked by striking differences during the early years of expansion. Whereas Leeds quickly became a railway crossroads of major trunk routes, events in Bradford tended to concentrate on building up a strong local network towards the Spen Valley, Shipley, Halifax, Keighley and Queensbury, and, of course, Leeds. The railway companies soon realised that Bradford was indeed a wealthy target and quickly provided most of the necessary services demanded by the city, but Bradford always had something of a branch line stigma which has resurfaced with a vengeance in more recent times. Happily, the latest developments to give rise to hopes that this unsatisfactory situation may finally be done away with in the next few years.

I hope this album will stimulate the reader to enquire further into the railway history of the two cities, since this is an area about which far more can be written than is contained within these covers. I have not given any details of the many wagon-ways or private lines which have existed in Leeds and Bradford, nor of the Middleton Railway which dates back to 1758. This brief history is concerned with what might be termed 'main line' developments, and the editorial considerations of time and space have imposed strict limitations on the album's content. I hope the purists will not be offended! My thanks go to all those who have assisted with the research material and supply of photographs, and particularly to Martin Bairstow, Douglas Butterfield, John Hodgson, Geoffrey Lewthwaite, Mike Mitchell and Trevor McKenna, who have all made personal contributions which have been especially helpful. Mr B. K. Cooper kindly allowed me to use material from his book *Titled Trains of Great Britain*, and the RCTS gave permission for reproduction of material from the *Railway Observer*.

Any manuscript of this length usually involves a typist with sore fingers and a wife who is often wondering where her 'other half' is about to disappear to next. This one is no exception, and I am sure that Mrs Linda Bradshaw will forever rue the day she allowed me to coax her out of retirement to produce another excellent manuscript from my awful scribble, whereas my wife Andrea has developed her mind-reading skills (usually triggered by my examination of the local weather conditions) to an uncanny degree. My thanks, yet again, to them both.

S. R. Batty
May 1988

1 The First Lines

The First Railway from Leeds

Although the centres of Leeds and Bradford are separated by hardly 10 miles, the early railway promoters of both cities were in no great hurry to construct a line between these two centres of swelling population and industrial growth. Bradford's woolmen wanted a connection to Manchester, whilst their Leeds counterparts urgently wanted to improve communications with Hull, the port which handled the city's booming woollen export trade to the European mainland. Bradford's surrounding ring of steep hills, with only one gap giving an easy access to the city (from the direction of Shipley and Bingley in the Aire Valley), was a daunting prospect to be faced by the early railway engineers. The hilly country between Bradford and the River Calder ensured that George Stephenson's Manchester & Leeds Railway (M&LR) came nowhere near the city as it swept along the valleys of the Aire and Calder between Leeds and Halifax. Bradford had to wait until the year 1850 before a connection was at last made into the Manchester & Leeds, and the city was eventually connected by railway to the centre of the cotton trade beyond the Pennine barrier. The level route to Shipley was utilised as part of the Leeds & Bradford Railway (L&BR), opened in 1846, but this was essentially only an extension of the Midland Railway's route from London and Derby to Leeds.

From Leeds eyes had turned towards the Mersey and the Humber as early as 1825 when

Left:
The L&S originally approached Leeds via a small, narrow tunnel at Richmond Hill. One of the original generator-equipped Class 47s, No 47407, passes the site with the 12.25 Newcastle-Liverpool on 24 August 1987. *S. R. Batty*

7

Marsh Lane station was the terminus of the L&S in Leeds. The site is now used for unloading stone by a cement company. Class 47 No 47411 passes by on 22 September 1987 with the 11.03 Liverpool-Newcastle train. *S. R. Batty*

a railway was proposed to be built from Liverpool and Manchester to Leeds and Hull. This ambitious scheme was itself predated by demands for a railway from Leeds to Selby in 1821. Both these early schemes failed due to the lack of expertise in building such extensive railway systems capable of handling large amounts of traffic and, more importantly, due to the tremendous power wielded by the canal companies which operated between these places. The roads had been in a desperate condition for decades, and this state of affairs was not helped by the canal companies gaining a powerful monopoly on the transport of raw materials and finished goods across the country from the Irish Sea to the North Sea. As well as exporting woollen goods via Hull, the Leeds mills also imported a great deal of raw wool through the port, and the sheer volume of this two-way trade with continental Europe had caused serious problems since the 1760s, when requests for improvements to the local canals and navigable rivers were first made. The Aire & Calder Navigation Co was, at the time, deemed to be a power in the land of almost equal standing to the monarchy, the Church, and the State. Difficult to imagine perhaps today, but this was an undisputed fact of industrial and commercial life in the West Riding of the 1820s. The Leeds and Selby scheme of 1821 was quietly killed off by the Aire & Calder Co, but they could not see that times were changing rapidly and it was now too late in the day for the canal companies to start making improvements which should have been carried out at least 20 years previously. The railway from Liverpool to Hull was initiated in 1825 under the direction of George Stephenson, who employed Joseph Locke to survey the Leeds-Hull section. Several inclined plans would have been used, but caution ruled the day and the Manchester-Hull section was abandoned until more experience of railway construction and operation could be gained, particularly as far as the Liverpool & Manchester Railway was concerned.

At this time the Aire & Calder Navigation was improved by the opening in 1826 of the Knottingley & Goole Canal, a development which speeded up the flow of goods between Leeds and Goole by avoiding the use of the twisting lower reaches of the Aire. But the canal company had been shaken by the strong demand for a railway to Hull, and in early 1825 there was talk of a completely new canal being cut from Selby to Leeds which would allow sea-going vessels to reach the very heart of the city. Locke's survey of 1825 was the spark which was needed to get the railway built from Leeds to Selby, and no amount of opposition from the canal owners could prevent the new scheme from going ahead. Trade between Leeds and Hull was never better, and the canals could not offer any improvements in transit times or haulage rates. Locke surveyed a route from Rhodes's tannery in Leeds to Halton, thence via an inclined plane to Micklefield, down another plane to Newthorpe, on to Milford and then down a third plane to Selby. Despite the inconvenience of the inclined planes this route was certainly direct and in 1827 a virtually identical one was proposed by Thomas Hill in a pamphlet entitled *A Treatise on the Leeds, Selby and Hull Railway*. Hill made several points regarding the poor service given by the canal owners. Hull was naturally the ultimate target of any railway to be built eastwards from Leeds, as the 60 miles between the cities could only be traversed either by impassable roads or by canals and rivers which were circuitous to say the least. The Ouse and Humber were strongly tidal rivers, but goods could be shipped between Hull or Goole and Selby if a good railway was built from there to Leeds. Selby was 30 miles from Leeds by canal and river, but only 20 miles by the proposed railway. Nine locks had to be negotiated, and Hill referred to the slowness of the journey quite succinctly; '... and, like all others subject to floods, frosts and draughts, frequent delays occur.'

Hill presented a well-reasoned and powerful argument for a Leeds and Selby railway, quoting the misdeeds of the canal owners and proposing a well-engineered length of railway, but his ideas for the means of propulsion to be employed really belonged to the early 18th rather than the early 19th century. Horses were to be used entirely throughout the line, mainly because locomotives required the use of inclined planes or a great deal of levelling, and also because horses did not need such strong track and could face a gradient of ½in/yd against 1in/15yd which he felt a locomotive was capable of. He admitted that the running cost of a locomotive would be far less than that for horses in terms of haulage capability, but felt that the capital cost was too high. He also stated, as if to crown his argument with one final, irrefutable point, that horses were *understood*! This priceless gem of irrelevance must have caused a few mouths to gape in Leeds, where the 40-year-old engineering industry was rapidly becoming a locomotive building centre for the entire country. Obviously horses were well understood, but early successes on colliery railways had very

Above:
**'B16/1' 4-6-0 No 61429 heads towards
Scarborough over the quadruple-track
approach to Crossgates with an excursion train
from Leeds in May 1955.** *C. Hogg*

clearly pointed in the direction that the future lay.

Hill estimated the cost of his horse-haulage system at £60,000 as against £140,000 for a system using locomotives, and also stated that railways generally would cost less than half the sum required to cut a canal and would be completed in about a third of the time.

By this time the Knottingley & Goole Canal was in operation, and many who had subscribed to the Liverpool-Leeds-Hull railway of three years earlier were alarmed at this development. The port of Goole began to expand rapidly and threatened to finish off Selby altogether, as a river port, in a very few years' time unless action was taken. James Walker of Leeds formally proposed the construction of the Leeds & Selby Railway (L&S) in 1829, following Locke's route of 1824 and using locomotive haulage throughout. The route was again surveyed and the proposals formally presented at a meeting in Selby during July 1829. Stephenson's original estimate of £200,000 was again quoted as the expected cost of the line, and the necessary capital was quickly raised, with most of the money coming from the Selby area and rather less than expected from the commercial interests of Leeds. However, the scheme was launched amidst an atmosphere of great confidence and healthy expectations for the new railway's future. The Bill was presented for the parliamentary session of 1829/30 and, despite the anticipated opposition of the canal owners and land owners along the route, the company received their Act on 29 May 1830, with an authorised capital of £210,000 and powers to borrow a further £90,000 if required. The first general meeting of the company was held in Selby during July 1830, under the Chairmanship of John Broadley. Walker & Burgess of London were appointed as civil engineers and, despite running across fairly level countryside, there was a great deal of engineering work to be done along the way, including 43 bridges, 43 occupational crossings, 16 level crossings and, of course, the 700yd Richmond Hill tunnel just to the east of the Leeds terminus. Looking at the opened-out site of this tunnel today, it is hard to imagine that the original bore was only 17ft high and 22ft wide. The stations at Marsh Lane, Leeds, and at Selby were built for £10,300 and £18,300

Above:
Many small collieries were served by the L&S between Leeds and Milford, but most of these disappeared and the bulk of the coal traffic then came from Gascoigne Wood yard. 'Q6' 0-8-0 No 63420 enters Crossgates on 17 August 1965 with a train of westbound wagons probably destined for Neville Hill sidings.
J. H. Cooper-Smith

respectively, but neither was provided with platforms — steps were to be used for gaining access to the trains.

Actual construction commenced on 1 October 1830, but delays regarding the exact siting of the Marsh Lane station led to little progress being made before early 1831. The location of the station led to some adverse comment, summed up in a local report of the time; '. . . in one of the most unpleasant and dirty, but likely soon to become one of the most improving parts of the town of Leeds.' Intermediate stations were built at Cross Gates, Garforth, Roman Road, Micklefield, Milford and Hambleton, and small collieries were to have access to the railway at Osmondthorpe, Manston, Garforth and Sutton. Once construction was under way the railway attracted a great deal of favourable comment for its excellent construction and undoubted commercial value. Even Thomas Hill was impressed for, after publishing a small pamphlet in 1829 recommending the use of stationary engines and inclined planes in order to cut down on the use of locomotives (which would present dire financial problems when the boilers and moving parts wore out), he again went into print in 1833 but in an entirely different vein. Gone was his obsession with horse power and also his commitment to

inclined planes, replaced by almost un-bounded enthusiasm for the new railway which was then well in progress. He stated that '. . . business upon it can be conducted in the best style, the completest work of the kind ever formed, and the repairs much less than upon any other line.'

Cloth was expected to be taken to Selby, and then on to Hull by river, within 13-14hr at a rate of 12s (60p)/ton, with a faster service being available (7½hr) for 16s (80p)/ton. Presumably the two rates were intended to reflect the difficulties which were expected to be caused by the state of the tides.

Richmond Hill tunnel (known today as Marsh Lane cutting) was the first in the world through which passengers were to be drawn by a steam locomotive, and several innovative measures were taken to ease the minds of

Right:
Low Moor station staff, 1921. *LYRS*

Below:
A special bound for the Yorkshire coast climbs through Osmondthorpe station behind 'B16/1' 4-6-0 No 61411 on 1 August 1960. *M. Mitchell*

Bottom:
Class 47 No 47418 speeds away from Crossgates with the 12.25 Newcastle-Liverpool on 6 August 1987. This section is now reduced to double-track only. *S. R. Batty*

passengers who would be nervous at the prospect of travelling for nearly half a mile at a depth of 80ft below ground behind a noisy, smoke-belching and dangerous steam contraption. Three shafts were used during the excavation, and these were left fully lined and open to the surface so that as much light as possible would penetrate the inky gloom. They could even be covered with glass, leaving a vent space above the shaft so that smoke could escape and rain could be kept out! The tunnel walls were whitewashed and mirrors, or 'plane reflectors' of 'tinned iron', were placed at the bottom of the shafts to spread as much illumination as possible. Initially passengers could read a newspaper as they passed through the tunnel, but problems in keeping the surfaces clean soon saw the idea abandoned, and oil lamps were placed in the carriages — but only during the darker months of the year!

Traffic on the route was expected to be heavy and, although the railway was constructed as a double-track system, sufficient land was purchased to allow two further tracks to be added if required in the future. The overbridges along the line were also built to span four tracks, and many of these particularly graceful structures remain today as a reminder of the L&S's foresight. Stone for building these bridges was expected to be found along the route as excavation took place, but this was not so and the materials were transported instead from Bramley Fall quarries, some miles away towards Bradford. The land at Richmond Hill was riddled with abandoned coal workings which caused more expense during the tunnelling work, and these two unforeseen items were largely responsible for pushing the cost of the railway up from the estimated £210,000 to £300,000.

By the time the L&S was nearing completion, the port developments which had taken place at Goole (by virtue of the Knottingley & Goole Canal) had had serious effects at Hull, where trade was declining. The L&S was expected to halt this decline by providing fast access from Leeds to Hull via Selby and the Ouse, but the real solution lay with the extension of the L&S to Hull, an event which was not to be fulfilled until 1 July 1840, perhaps the most significant date in the railway history of the West Riding of Yorkshire.

But back to Marsh Lane. The public opening date was fixed for 22 September 1834, and single fares of 3s (15p) first-class and 2s (10p) second-class were to be levied. To accommodate the tide at Selby, an early departure of the first train from Leeds was set at 06.00 in order

that the return departure could be made after the arrival of the steamer from Hull at about 11.00. Four days before this, the customary directors' trip along the line was made by Benjamin Gott, Edward Baines MP, John Wilson, Newman Cash, Henry Marshall, S. W. Waude and engineer John Walker. Amidst thousands of spectators they left Leeds at 11.00, and returned from Selby at 17.00 for a 2hr journey back to Leeds. The prime purpose was to make sure the line was indeed fit for use. Only one line was laid in places, and they agreed that this might cause some delay. Two lines were expected to be in use throughout by the end of the year, and they decided to withhold the carriage of goods until 15 December, which was to be regarded as the 'official' opening date when the line was fully available for the carriage of all goods traffic. Nevertheless, the railway was deemed 'a far superior work of art' than any other of its kind, with a 'very favourable appearance' throughout and the 'great embankments' at Halton and Milford particularly attracted favourable comment. The contractors responsible were Hamer & Pratt of Goole and Nowell & Son of Dewsbury. The trip took place in four open coaches hauled by the locomotive *Nelson*, built by the Leeds firm of Fenton, Murray & Jackson, and passed without incident. This locomotive had been delivered (or 'launched', to use the contemporary expression) from the foundry on 5 September for a trial run the following day, but no details of this exercise were reported. *Nelson* was reckoned to be equivalent in haulage ability to 18-20 horses!

On the great day itself, no display was provided at Leeds due to the early hour set for departure. This was delayed until 06.30, when the 150 passengers in three first-class carriages (named *Juno, Vesta* and *Diana*) and four open carriages struggled away behind *Nelson*. Overnight rain and early morning dampness caused the rails to be very slippery, and *Nelson* was soon to be heard 'groaning like an elephant'. The first hour saw only 4½ miles covered, with the aid of ashes liberally sprinkled on the rails, but provided a spectacle for 20,000 people in the Halton area. Progress then improved, the run to Selby taking a further 45min for an arrival at about 09.00. Here the commotion was great indeed, with the usual crowds cheering and waving and flags flying everywhere — someone even found a few cannons to fire off. The return departure took place at 11.15 with arrival at Leeds by 12.30. Speeds of up to 27mph were reached by Milford, dropping to 13mph to Micklefield but increasing to 30mph over the last seven miles

Above:
Shipley (Bradford Junction), 24 July 1965.
D. Butterfield

from Brown Moor. The crowds had also increased, to somewhere between 40-50,000, and the railway police must have had a hard time keeping control and trying to signal the passage of the train. Many of the crowds turned up at Marsh Lane station hoping for a ride, but they were told to return home as no more trains were to run on that day. Two trains were, however, to be sent on all following days, to meet the tides at Selby. The next day's morning train took only 65min, and the second train left at 14.30 but came to grief at Garforth where *Nelson's* regulator rod broke and could not be repaired. After waiting for an hour, horses were used to drag the train to Leeds, which was eventually reached at 21.00. Thomas Hill may have smiled at this, and he would surely have been interested to read, in the *Leeds Mercury*, that whilst the cows in the lineside fields ran away from the new trains, the horses completely ignored the entire spectacle!

Between 22 and 25 September, 1,522 passengers were carried and £178 taken in fares, and the trains settled down to regular departures from Leeds at 06.00 and 14.00 and from Selby

at 12.30 and 16.30. Marsh Lane station was indeed generally thought to be in need of improvement. To be fair to the L&S, it seems that the company had to make do with this site as being the best they could get at the time. Press reports of the day state that a station was originally wanted in School Close, where a sharing arrangement was to be made with a proposed Leeds and Bradford railway. This later scheme failed, and the L&S had to look elsewhere. As far as traffic was concerned, the outlook was healthy. Goods took 3hr to reach Selby by road, and this would be reduced to 1hr by the time the line was ready to handle freight trains. Some 1,200 tons/week were expected to be sent from Manchester to Hull, at a rate of 36s-40s (£1.80-£2)/ton, and the rates and service would improve in the years ahead when more railways were built, particularly between Manchester and Leeds and Hull and Selby. As mentioned earlier, the company had purchased sufficient land to allow quadruple track to be laid if required in the future and this allowed the two lines to be generously spaced at 6ft 6in apart, some 18in greater separation than had been used on the Liverpool & Manchester Railway (L&MR).

The early years of the L&S were profitable, with traffic increasing fivefold by 1836. Nine new locomotives were ordered in 1839 from Kirtley & Co of Warrington for use on passenger trains. Earlier locomotives had also been supplied by Kirtley's, along with examples from Fenton, Murray & Jackson of Leeds, and all carried names such as *Hawk*, *Dart*, *Express*, *Lord Hood*, *Swallow*, and, of course, *Nelson*. They were capable of speeds of up to 25mph, and double-heading was often used on the gradient from Milford to Garforth.

But hard times soon befell the L&S, due to the vigorous competition put up by the Aire & Calder Navigation along their routes to Goole and Selby. The Hull & Selby Railway (H&SR) opened on 1 July 1840, but other events of this significant date cast a long shadow over the future of the L&S. George Hudson's York & North Midland Railway (Y&NMR) opened from York to Altofts Junction, where it met the simultaneously-opened North Midland Railway (NMR) from Derby to Leeds. A spur had been built to connect the Y&NMR and L&S at Milford, and this was opened by May 1839 being followed by a second connection, from the opposite direction of the Y&NMR, on 9 November 1840. By July 1840 another spur had been built from Methley Junction, on the NMR, to Whitwood Junction, near Castleford, on the Y&NMR. Hudson realised that he could use these lines to compete for the Leeds-Selby-

Above:
The Aire Valley offered an easy route from Leeds to Shipley and thence to Bradford via the only natural gap in the hills which surround the city. Stanier Class '5' 4-6-0 No 44828 passes Leeds Junction with a St Pancras express on 19 April 1960. *D. Butterfield*

Hull traffic and acted with great speed to gobble up any competition. He first proposed that his NMR trains from Leeds to Selby should run along the L&S alternately with those of the parent company, but the L&S directors would not agree. The travelling public were not too keen on using Hudson's roundabout route, which was 4½ miles longer and involved changing trains at York Junction (now Gascoigne Wood). Hudson then put a very tempting offer on the table — he would lease the L&S for 31 years at an annual rental of £17,000, with a built-in option of outright purchase. The hard-up directors could not refuse such an offer, and duly agreed. Hudson sprang his trap on 9 November 1840, when the lease came into effect and the south-to-east curve from Milford to York Junction was opened. He closed the L&S to passenger traffic from Leeds to York Junction, thus ensuring that all York and Hull passengers had to travel via the Y&NMR, with Hull passengers having to change at the remote and exposed junction.

Thus, Hudson had killed off his competition, relegated a finely-engineered railway to little more than a goods branch line, and caused a great deal of hostility in Leeds. Freight traffic was carried until 1848, when it too was diverted via Methley and Whitwood into the Hudson empire. Some local passenger traffic between Milford and Leeds resumed from 1850, but the important through trains were not to reappear for nearly 30 years after withdrawal. Hudson exercised his option of purchase on 23 May 1844, buying out the L&S

for £365,000 and so killing off, in practical and commercial terms, the first passenger-carrying locomotive-worked railway out of Leeds.

Linking Leeds with Bradford

To build a railway between these two large cities separated by only 9½ miles would not, apparently, seem to be a difficult task in terms of railway engineering. The city of Bradford lay within a large bowl-shaped depression surrounded by hills on all but the northern side, and this easy exit had already been used to build a short canal to meet the Leeds & Liverpool Canal at Shipley. Although leaving in the wrong direction, this exit would then allow an easy approach to Leeds along the Aire Valley, where the extra mileage involved would be compensated for by the lack of gradients to be found along the route via Shipley and Kirkstall. The shorter, direct east-west route from Leeds meant some climbing from Leeds and a ravine-like approach into Bradford, but the journey was some four miles shorter than by the Aire Valley route.

Above:
Work on the L&BR started at Thackley tunnel in 1844. Class 144 DMU No 144014 leaves the 1901-built bore with the 11.39 Skipton-Leeds on 22 September 1987. *S. R. Batty*

These options and constraints were well recognised when the earliest railway proposals were formulated for the Bradford area in the early 1830s. The first scheme was drawn up in 1830 to reach Leeds via Stanningley (ie the 'Short' line) and join up with the L&S at a point near Neville Hill, so giving access to Hull via the River Ouse. This was opposed and dropped, but two years later reappeared as part of a Leeds-Bradford-Halifax-Manchester railway in which atmospheric propulsion was to be used between the two cities. Lack of support caused this idea to fail also and nothing more was done until 1838. It was during the mid-1830s that Bradfordians realised that the new railway age apparently had little time for their city, and this belief was confirmed when George Stephenson engineered the newly-created M&LR's main line along the valley of the Calder, several miles to the south and with no intention

whatsoever of providing any communication at all to Bradford. This was seen as a gross insult to the city, especially after the 1832 proposals had come to naught. The Calder Valley offered a natural path for a railway across the Pennines (and was certainly more suitable than any route offered by the Aire Valley via Shipley and Skipton), even though the M&LR was to bypass such large centres as Bradford and Huddersfield. Many smaller towns were to be served, such as Hebden Bridge, Sowerby Bridge, Elland, Brighouse, Mirfield, Dewsbury, Wakefield and Normanton, but the hilly country between Bradford and the Calder was, to Stephenson, as impenetrable as the Alps would have been. An early protagonist for both a Leeds-Bradford and a Bradford-Manchester railway had been Thomas Hill, the pamphleteer of the early L&S days. In 1833 Hill published a short essay entitled *A Short Treatise on Rail Roads*, in which he complained bitterly about the extortionate charges made by canal owners and also about the apparent lack of local effort which had led to the loss of the 1830 Leeds-Bradford and 1832 Leeds-Bradford-Manchester schemes. He proposed a Manchester and Leeds railway to follow the Calder

Valley (this was three years before the M&LR was eventually incorporated, but three years also after the route had first been surveyed), but with a branch trailing in at Brighouse from Bradford via Wibsey, Bierley, Wyke and Bailiff Bridge, the entire scheme being built for £3,000-£4,000/mile. He reserved his strongest criticism for the failure of any company to build a Leeds-Stanningley-Bradford railway, which he reckoned should cost £45,000 for the 9½-mile route:

'There is not a greater absurdity in the commercial and scientific world, nor a greater proof of human weakness and imbecility, than that the Inhabitants of Bradford and its Vicinity, abounding with population, minerals and trade, should be blind to the advantages of railroad conveyance, as above stated, as well as their individual benefit as traders and subscribers.'

Thus by 1838 the M&LR and the NMR (from Derby to Leeds) were both well underway. A little further afield were to be seen such railways as the L&MR, the L&S and the infant Y&NM and the H&SR. Bradford was losing out in all directions, and future developments from 1838 took place against a background of increasing competition between the M&LR and NMR. The Leeds & Bradford Railway (L&BR) was not destined to be opened until 1846, by which time what should have been a fairly straightforward railway project had become embroiled within the politics and machinations of all those who, by then, were quite willing (on paper at least) to lay railway lines along any small valley they could get their contractors into.

In 1838, when he was busy with the construction of the M&LR, Stephenson was approached by parties from Leeds and Bradford and asked to survey a route between the towns. Naturally, he favoured the Aire Valley route which would progress from Leeds to Shipley before turning southwards towards Bradford along the easiest entry to the centre of the town. Lack of speculators (and their capital) doomed the scheme to failure, and the rather depressed state of the economy thereafter saw no further railway promotion until

the year 1842. The M&LR had opened throughout in 1841, with Bradford being connected by a coach to Brighouse, and in the following year a party from Halifax requested the M&LR to build a line from their main line through Halifax to Bradford, rather than make do with the simple Halifax branch line which was already under construction. The Manchester company would have none of this, and a further request in 1843 met with a similar fate. By now, the railway promoters of Bradford had had enough of the M&LR, and cast their eyes again towards Leeds, where the NMR was doing very nicely and was set to become an influential partner of the soon-to-be-formed Midland Railway (MR). George Hudson, the NMR chairman, and Robert Stephenson were both approached for help. Robert Stephenson stuck by his father's proposals of 1838, and Hudson quickly grabbed his chance to make sure his company was the first to strike into the heartland of the West Riding. The NMR preferred to concentrate instead on the amalgamation issues which led to the formation of the MR in 1844, and deferred the scheme, but the wily Hudson

went ahead on his own and formed the Leeds & Bradford Railway Co. The L&BR was put before Parliament in 1844, following the Aire Valley route, and the M&LR immediately took fright at the prospect of such powerful competition (the L&BR was clearly a progeny of the MR, whose system it was intended to join at Leeds), and suddenly offered a route from their main line to Bradford which completely ignored the efforts of all parties over the previous years of wrangling. Ignoring the wishes of Halifax to be connected with Bradford and apparently aiming instead at the future Leeds-Bradford traffic, the M&LR proposed a hastily-conceived scheme known as the Ledgard Bridge branch, leaving their main line at Mirfield and reaching Bradford via Cleckheaton. The curves were gentle, but the gradients were fearsome indeed, reaching an inclination of 1 in 30 from Mirfield and almost 1 in 25 on the descent from Bierley to Bradford centre. Cable haulage would be required at both ends of the line, a feature which was certainly considered undesirable by 1844, regardless of gradients.

Both the Ledgard Bridge and L&BR schemes

went to Parliament together in 1844. The former was thrown out by virtue of its gradients and opposition from the L&BR and also from the bypassed town of Halifax, but the L&BR scheme did not sail through unhindered. Many backers of the earlier 'short-line' schemes opposed the Aire Valley route, still maintaining that any railway between the cities should go via Stanningley, and this opposition caused some difficulty in Parliament. As events turned out, the L&BR was let off the hook, but they had to agree to build on from Bradford via Halifax to the M&LR at Sowerby Bridge, so satisfying the persistent outcry which had come from Halifax since the earliest M&LR days. One particularly interesting point which emerged at this time concerned a direct railway from Halifax to Bradford which had been surveyed by one Richard Carter. Carter planned a route which was very close to today's railway via Low Moor, after initially surveying, but then rejecting, a route via Thornton (the latter was eventually opened, on a similar route, 35 years afterwards). Carter also wished to build towards the M&LR at Luddendenfoot, so

saving nearly 10 miles to Manchester compared to the Mirfield route, but all his schemes were crushed by the M&LR opposition.

Having received assent for their Aire Valley route, the L&BR then formed a new company, the West Yorkshire Railway (WYR), to build the line to Sowerby Bridge and also three other lines in the West Riding. These were:

1 From Low Moor, on the planned Bradford-Halifax line, to the proposed Leeds, Dewsbury & Manchester Railway (LD&MR) near Mirfield, and routed via Cleckheaton and the Spen Valley.

2 From Heckmondwike (on the Spen Valley route) to the M&LR at Thornhill, via Ravensthorpe.

3 From the WYR Bradford-Halifax line at Bowling to Wortley Junction, Leeds, on the L&BR and LD&MR. This would have threaded the Tong Valley between Leeds and Bradford.

The M&LR now felt threatened indeed, and began to see that after ignoring years of opportunity for getting established in the West Riding, there was now a distinct possibility that they would never achieve any expansion away from their main line along the Calder and Aire Valleys to Wakefield and Leeds. In November 1844 the M&LR produced plans for the Leeds & West Riding Junction Railway (L&WRJR), a company which was to build similar railways to those planned by the WYR and also whose chairman happened to hold the same position on the M&LR. Perhaps to try and steal the initiative from the WYR when both schemes went to Parliament, the L&WRJR planned to build further short lines as well as those which were almost identical to the WYR lines. These additional schemes were:

1 From Pickle Bridge, Wyke to Anchor Pit on the MLR main line near Bradley Wood.
2 Wortley-Morley-Dewsbury, with a branch from Batley to Gomersal.
3 Halifax-Brighouse-Cooper Bridge-Huddersfield.

Thus, by 1845 the populace of the Leeds, Bradford and Halifax areas and the Calder and Spen Valleys were being deluged with railway proposals — a far cry from events of 2 years previously. The principal schemes of the two companies were almost identical for the simple reason that the L&WRJR had employed a surveyor who had been party to the original WYR. Richard Carter, mentioned previously for his pre-1844 surveys between Halifax and Bradford, was subsequently employed by the WYR to survey their planned lines in the Spen Valley and from Bowling to Wortley. He had been assisted by John Leather, who was therefore familiar with all the work undertaken by Carter for the WYR. At this point the 'short line' party, aggrieved at losing out to the L&BR, entered the scene once more. They had thrown in their lot with the M&LR, seeing the L&WRJR as the only possible way of getting their railway built. John Leather was employed as surveyor to the L&WRJR, and so was able to provide almost instant plans for the new company. But the M&LR had a tough time in the latter half of 1844, despite opening a branch line to Halifax and trying to reassure everyone that the L&WRJR would eventually provide an excellent service to all in the West Riding. George Stephenson did not believe that the M&LR had good intentions for Yorkshire, saying that their only goal was to connect Manchester with the North Sea and that they should not meddle in West Riding affairs. John Gott, member of a well-known Leeds family and a railway promoter of the Riding, observed that there was no Leeds money in the

M&LR — it should be called 'the Manchester', as it was run by Manchester men for their own benefit, with no thought given for the needs of the woollen towns of Yorkshire. The M&LR standards of service were appalling, with ambiguous fare tables, poor train services, bad connections, primitive passenger facilities and staff whose attitudes to the public varied between indifference and downright hostility. Their Ledgard Bridge branch — proposed in opposition to the L&BR — was thrown out during the late summer, and the L&BR celebrated this in October, looking forward to a similar defeat for the L&WRJR scheme in the 1845 session. They viewed this as a hopeless scheme salvaged from the remains of the Ledgard Bridge line, but the L&BR was too short-sighted. Robert Stephenson, their engineer, was more realistic and pointed out that two schemes as similar as those of the WYR and the L&WRJR going to Parliament would certainly both be rejected. He was to be proved correct, but this was not the end of the story by a long way.

The 1845 Parliamentary session was a busy one indeed, and an early casualty was the WYR Bill, which was rejected on 9 May. Apart from failing on the technical matter of not satisfying the preliminary stage, it was simply outgunned by the greater capital of the M&LR and the apparently more comprehensive network proposed by the L&WRJR scheme (it must be remembered that despite having close links with the recently formed MR, the L&BR was nevertheless still a small, local, independent company which had to stand on its own feet and could not call on its mighty neighbour in Leeds for help). The L&WRJR now felt sure of success, but they had aroused powerful opposition from other companies and soon saw their Bill also rejected, just as Robert Stephenson had predicted. The LD&MR objected to the planned Wortley-Dewsbury line, and the Huddersfield & Manchester Railway (H&MR) objected to the Brighouse-Cooper Bridge-Huddersfield section, which competed directly with their own planned junction to the LD&MR. These routes had already been approved by Parliament, and the L&WRJR came to agreement over running powers into Leeds in return for dropping its planned Wortley-Dewsbury branch, but all to no avail. On many points the L&WRJR was thought to be a better scheme than the WYR, but they also failed on one other crucial matter. The WYR had produced plans for a junction in Bradford between the L&BR and the proposed new railways, but they had kept the details so closely guarded that the L&WRJR had been

Above:
Leeds (Wellington) station was opened in 1846 and was quickly rebuilt by 1853. Fairburn '4MT' 2-6-4T No 42139 waits to depart with a Bradford train from the 1938-rebuilt station on 21 October 1962. *J. S. Whiteley*

unable to provide any similar plans for a junction with their own lines. Even with Leather's help, the M&LR could not find sufficient information about the L&BR Bradford line to plan any sort of cross-town railway or junction. Railway communication from Bradford onwards to Halifax had been a vital condition of the L&BR obtaining their Bill, and Parliament was not going to entertain any opposing scheme which could not satisfy this point. Both schemes were therefore lost, and Bradfordians suddenly found that where two companies had been vying for the powers to put their city well and truly on the railway map, now there were none — for the time being at least. Also lost was the first chance of a railway connection across the town centre, plans for which would reoccur several times over the following 75 years or so, and which are still under discussion some 145 years after this first scheme was proposed.

Taking Robert Stephenson's advice, the defeated companies decided to amalgamate before reapplying to Parliament in the 1846 Session. This marriage of two previously-opposed companies was brought about not just by Stephenson's advice, but also by similar overtures being made by the M&LR to the L&BR. Such an alliance would eventually have given the M&LR another route into Leeds, via the former L&WRJR/WYR lines and the L&BR via Shipley. The L&BR initially accepted the M&LR plan, and the L&WRJR and WYR then joined forces to become the West Riding Union Railway (WRUR), in which the M&LR was the dominant partner with responsibility for all the planned works. The WRUR was to build the lines previously proposed, but also with some additional ones;

1 Wyke-Brighouse
2 Salter Hebble-Elland-Huddersfield
3 From Stanningley, on the Bowling-Wortley line, to Gildersome on a planned Leeds, Dewsbury and Huddersfield Railway (LD&HR) branch.

The L&BR agreed to build a cross-town line from a junction at Manningham to join the

Above:
Clear road ahead as 'Patriot' 4-6-0 No 45513 passes Wortley Junction with the 13.54 Leeds-Carnforth on 7 June 1961. *G. W. Morrison*

WRUR at Well Street, so completing a railway loop between Leeds and Bradford. All these matters went to Parliament in 1846, and the Acts were approved for the WRUR formation and for the L&BR junction line to the new company, but the Bill for amalgamation of the M&LR and L&BR — perhaps 'takeover' would have been a better expression — failed. The L&BR claimed the agreement to be too much in favour of the M&LR interests, and the two companies soon fell out over the affair, despite having apparently discussed the matter to everyone's satisfaction at the end of 1845. The L&BR withdrew from the proposal in June 1846, abandoned the agreed cross-town line, almost before the ink was dry on the Act, and quickly entered a leasing agreement with Hudson's MR. Five years later the L&BR was purchased outright by the MR, but the

cross-town line never appeared — much to the chagrin of the MR in later years.

The bright spot of 1846 was undoubtedly the opening the L&BR for public use on 1 July. Work had started immediately the Act was passed on 4 July 1844 and had progressed well, with Thackley tunnel being the major engineering work involved. From Market Street in Bradford the line reached out to Shipley before turning generally eastwards to Leeds via Kirkstall and Holbeck, terminating in the excellently-sited Wellington station placed right in the heart of the city. A connection was built to allow the MR to extend their line to the new station from their original terminus in Hunslet, and this was brought into use from 1 July. As was the custom of the times the formal opening was preceded by the contractor's special, which ran no less than a full month before the public opening. On 30 May a return train left Leeds at 13.00, to the strains of two bands on board the train who also played at Wellington station and afterwards at the White Horse Inn in Boar Lane. The locomotives used were *Lindsay* on the outward trip and *Stephenson* on the return,

Class '4MT' 2-6-4T No 42072 departs from the Wellington platforms with a lengthy Sheffield train during the early 1960s. *E. Treacy*

and both were decorated with flags and flowers and two headboards — one being the usual 'See the Conquering Hero Comes' and the other simply asking 'Who'd have thought it?' This latter must have been prompted by the thought, then held by many, that such an essential railway should have been built at least 10 years previously. There were no intermediate stations along the way at the time, and no cheering took place at Bradford due to a severe economic depression which had hit the city (several cannon were fired as the trains passed Kirkstall Forge, though). The day of the formal opening, 30 June, was declared a public holiday in Bradford, and spirits were high despite the economic gloom and poor weather. Over 2,000 people, including the entire Leeds Corporation, were invited to the festivities held at each end of the line. One train left Bradford at 11.00 to get people to Leeds in time for a ceremonial departure at 12.00, but this was delayed until 13.14. By this time the new Wellington station was packed with more than 50 carriages, of NMR and Y&NMR ownership, and no less than three trains were made up for the 1hr run to Bradford. George Hudson travelled in the second train, and the entire party had lunch in a pavilion erected outside Market Street station. The return later in the afternoon was much brisker, taking only 35min. All the works along the line were of a very plain nature, as the speed of construction had allowed no time for fanciful touches to stonework by the contractors involved. The contractors had been Crawshaw's from Leeds to Kirkstall, Tredwell's from Kirkstall to Thackley, Nowell & Hattersley at Thackley tunnel (where work had started), and James Bray from Thackley into Bradford. The civil engineering work also involved rock cuttings at Armley and near Horsforth, a viaduct at Apperley Bridge, six bridges over the Aire and four over the Leeds & Liverpool Canal. After the Leeds arrival (again heralded by a cannonade at Kirkstall) a celebration dinner was provided at the Music Hall.

2 Early West Riding Developments

The Downfall of Hudson

The L&BR was destined to exist independently for only five years after opening, due to its particularly attractive prospect for certain other railway companies. It was also to play a leading role on the stage of George Hudson's downfall from railway power. The lucrative possibilities of extending the railway along the Aire Valley, instead of just making a sharp turn at Shipley, had long been obvious to the original promoters and by September of 1844 plans were laid to reach out through Bingley, Keighley and Skipton to a junction with the East Lancashire Railway (ELR) at Colne. Keighley was reached by March 1847 and Colne during the following year. By 1849 further lines built in Lancashire allowed the L&BR and ELR to offer a Leeds-Liverpool route which was highly competitive with the former M&LR (now Lancashire & Yorkshire Railway) route via the Calder Valley. Seeing these developments in the near future, both the M&LR and the ELR offered to lease the L&BR.

The MR was compelled to enter the fray, not just to keep the M&LR out but also to capture a route to Carlisle and Scotland via the L&BR extended line's junction with the 'Little North Western' route beyond Skipton. The L&BR did not want to be captured by the M&LR, so consequently consented to a leasing agreement with the Midland only three weeks after the public opening, in July 1846. The Midland's route to the northwest was thus secured, but Hudson's continued attempts to gain total control of the L&BR led to his fall. In early 1849, as chairman of the L&BR, he led a meeting of the MR, of which he was also chairman, and argued in favour of the Midland buying out the L&BR — his own company. This was seen as a flagrant case of a railway magnate using his position of power in two companies in order to line his own pockets, and uproar followed. He should not have taken any part in the meeting at all, but by speaking up he brought disgrace upon himself. He resigned as chairman of the MR on 17 April 1849, was then expelled from the L&BR, and had lost all his railway powers by May of the same year. Fifteen years to build an empire, two weeks to lose it.

The original leasing agreement of 1846 guaranteed the L&BR shareholders a dividend

Below:
Liversedge (Central) station on 2 October 1966, looking towards Low Moor. *D. Butterfield*

of 10% from the MR. By August 1850 the MR shareholders were receiving only 2% from their investments, due mainly to severe competition from the embryo Great Northern Railway (GNR). To get out of this embarrassing situation the MR sought to abandon the lease altogether, but the directors thought that such a move would not only blacken their own characters but would also badly shake the confidence of all investors in railway property. They had no choice but to buy out the L&BR completely, and a Bill was duly approved for this purpose in 1851. The shareholders gave their approval on 4 June, and the L&BR became a small part of the Midland empire. Their route to the north was thus secured, but providing a decent train service to Bradford from London and the Midlands was to be a thorn in their side for many a year.

The West Riding Union Lines

The WRUR Bill was sent to Parliament in June 1846, and the Act was passed during the following August. Authorised capital of £2 million was allowed, with powers to borrow another £666,666 to build 45 miles of railway.

1 Leeds-Bradford-Halifax via Bowling (including the 'Short line')
2 Bradford-Low Moor-Halifax
3 Low Moor-Mirfield
4 Thornhill-Cleckheaton-Heckmondwike
5 Halifax-Huddersfield via Salter Hebble.

A connecting branch to Gildersome was also to be built from Low Moor. The WRUR was an ambitious scheme, and many felt the M&LR had no intention of completing it, especially as one of the conditions placed on the Act was that the WRUR should be incorporated with the M&LR within three months of the passing

of the Act. The Manchester company thus had total control of the scheme, and could pull out at any time they wished.

Construction work was started on 21 October 1846 when the Hon C. Wood, a local MP, cut the first turf at Halifax with the assistance of John Hawkshaw, the line's engineer, and Lord Morpeth, one of the M&LR's founder members. During the next month the WRUR was taken over by the M&LR and in the following year the latter became the Lancashire & Yorkshire Railway (LYR) — the same company with a different name and also with the same fickle attitude towards West Riding railways. The engineering work involved in building the WRUR lines was responsible for rather slow progress and, in April 1848, the LYR applied for a two-year extension of the construction period. The first line to open was the Mirfield-Low Moor branch along the Spen Valley, which included two short tunnels at Liversedge and Low Moor. Gradients were not too steep, with stretches of 1 in 100 north of Heckmondwike station. A directors' opening day was held on 12 July 1848, when a train of 30 carriages hauled by four locomotives travelled up and down the line throughout the day for the benefit of almost 300 passengers. After a cold collation at Cleckheaton, the directors left for Manchester and Leeds at about 19.00, but the Leeds party was delayed — it was, after all, the LYR's main line upon which they had to travel

Below:
A local freight arrives at Cleckheaton (Central) behind Stanier '8F' 2-8-0 No 48278. Part of this site is now occupied by a supermarket and car park. *D. I. Wood*

— and did not arrive until the small hours of the following day. Public opening followed on 18 July with 12 trains daily each way along the branch. Stagecoaches ceased running from Bradford to Mirfield, but continued to run to Low Moor.

Tunnelling work caused more delay on the other lines and it was not until May 1850 that the section from Low Moor into Bradford was completed. The line was due to be inspected by Capt Leffen, the Board of Trade's Inspector of Railways, on 8 May, but some consternation greeted his non-arrival at Low Moor at the appointed time of 13.00. He had still failed to appear by 14.30, so the assembled directors in their three-coach train set off for a ride to Bradford (where the station was incomplete), probably to pass the time and decide what to do next. Fortunately, upon their return to Low Moor for a rather late lunch, Capt Leffen had arrived after being badly delayed at Liverpool. He passed the line as fit for use and the first services began on 9 May, with an express arriving at Bradford at 10.30 complete with the usual decoration and flags. A large crowd had gathered at the station (known then as Bradford L&Y, and Bradford Exchange from April 1867), most of whom were glad to see an end to omnibus travel to Low Moor. The line from Halifax to Low Moor was opened on 7 August without any ceremony, despite the fact that Bradford now had a direct route to Manchester after four long years of construction work by Miller and Blackie. Perhaps the reason for the lack of celebration lay in the

LYR's attitude towards Bradford generally. They made no secret of their view of the Bradford line as being one of secondary importance, and still many people feared that the LYR would leave the city in the lurch with poor railways and services. Very soon after the opening of the Halifax-Bradford line, the LYR announced that it would not proceed with any more WRUR lines, and abandoned the Thornhill-Heckmondwike spur, the Salter Hebble line and, most important of all, the Bowling-Wortley line and the branch to Gildersome. Argument continued throughout 1850 and Parliamentary action was taken against the LYR in 1851 to make them complete the works, but the company successfully appealed against this measure. Part of the WRUR Act of 1846 had ensured that the L&BR would not lose money when the WRUR line from Leeds to Bradford was built, and this was to be done by making the WRUR — really the LYR — pay an agreed part of their profits to the L&BR. The LYR argued, quite fairly, that they would be paying money to a company which had no part in the construction of the WRUR lines and, in 1852, they obtained powers to abandon the remaining unbuilt WRUR lines.

The 'Short Line'

By this time the 'Short line' protagonists were determined that they would have their railway with or without the help or hindrance of the LYR and, in November 1851, they quickly

Far left:
The remains of Liversedge (Central) in October 1987, looking towards Mirfield. The track, disused for six years, remains as part of the proposed West Yorkshire Transport Museum.
S. R. Batty

Above and left:
Surprisingly, the station footbridge remains intact at Heckmondwike (Central). The approaches lead to nowhere, the bridge spans a derelict area and nature is reclaiming the staircases.
S. R. Batty

Above:
The exterior of the LBHJR Adolphus Street terminus in Bradford, described in 1854 as 'Italianate' in appearance. Brickwork chimney stacks had appeared by 1956! *K. Field*

Right:
The generous interior accommodation is apparent in this view of the building taken in September 1956. Note the continental ferry vans and large bales of wool. Adolphus Street closed in 1972. *K. Field*

Below right:
Fowler 2-6-4T No 42406 nears Laisterdyke with the 15.09 Bradford-King's Cross on 28 July 1964. *M. Mitchell*

Far right:
A 'Calder Valley' DMU climbs out of Bradford towards Laisterdyke on 4 February 1967. The LBHJR line to Bowling and Halifax is visible on the left, and the approaches to the original station at Adolphus Street can be seen bearing to the right. *L. A. Nixon*

formed their own company to build a line from Leeds to Bradford via Stanningley and also connecting with the Bradford-Halifax line at Bowling. The company was known as the Leeds, Bradford & Halifax Junction Railway (LBHJR) and John Hawkshaw, late of the WRUR, was engaged as engineer. The LBHJR hoped to build only about 7½ miles of railway, hoping to get running powers over the Leeds, Dewsbury & Manchester section of the LNWR from Leeds to Wortley Junction and over the LYR from Bowling to Halifax. Bradford was to be served by a third terminal station, built in Adolphus and Dryden Streets and reached by a branch of the railway from Laister Dyke (Laisterdyke in later years) on the line to Bowling. These proposals were all accepted by Parliament and the Act was passed on 30 June 1852, from which date also the LYR were given running powers over the new line, and the infant GNR was engaged to operate it upon completion. So began the GNR's long association with the West Riding, and its penetration of the area by the simple expedient of buying up local railway companies formed to build small pieces of railway between adjacent towns.

No great engineering difficulties were encountered and the line was opened for passenger traffic from 1 August 1854 and for goods traffic on 7 August. The intermediate stations were not yet ready and any goods traffic to Bradford would have to use LYR facilities. Adolphus Street station was a considerable distance out of the town centre and involved an uphill climb for any intending travellers. It too was incomplete, and a temporary station was provided until completion of the building in June 1855. Much of this protracted delay was due to a collapse of the roof which took place in late 1854. The station's location was too off-putting for many

travellers, and the rival MR route continued to flourish so well that the LBHJR directors quickly decided to extend their line down into the LYR station in the town centre. Parliament took more than a little convincing of the proposed line's merits, and finally agreed to the scheme in 1864 after initially rejecting the idea in 1859. Adolphus Street was generally thought to have been a well-designed and laid-out building well suited to the traffic demands and giving a good standard of comfort to its users, but its poor location ensured that its days as a passenger terminus were numbered. The new link line was to be laid from Hammerton Street Junction, on the

LBHJR Laister Dyke-Adolphus Street branch, to Mill Lane Junction on the LYR Bradford-Halifax line. Although it was only ¾-mile in length, some fearsome excavation was required and the line was not ready for opening until January 1867, by which time the LBHJR had been wholly owned by the GNR for two years.

But back to 1 August 1854, and the first day of business on the long-awaited 'Short line' which had been so eagerly sought after by the cloth manufacturers of the Stanningley and Pudsey areas. Those travelling on the first train — there was no ceremony at all, the line simply opened for traffic as if it had done so on

every preceding day for years past — encountered what could only be called a shambles. The first train was due to depart from Stanningley at 08.52 for an arrival at Leeds Central at 09.10, but delays managed to put the Stanningley departure back to 09.20. Consequently, with business starting at the Leeds Cloth Market at 09.30, there was a stampede to get out of Central station and away to the town as quickly as possible after eventual arrival at just before 10.00, 50min late. At this time the carriages of arriving trains were detached from the locomotive outside the station and then allowed to freewheel into the station under the control of a brakeman, and this little operation apparently caused great delay. The solitary ticket collector was overwhelmed, and he probably hoped that many of the travellers would indeed take up their threat to revert to using the roads if nothing was done to improve matters. Travel towards Bradford was discouraged because no trains called at the intermediate stations (Holbeck, Armley & Wortley, Bramley, Stanningley and Laister Dyke) in that direction between the hours of 08.30 and 11.30, which was no use for anyone wanting to attend the Bradford markets. For some strange reason, passengers from Leeds to Stanningley were charged 6d for a third-class ticket, but those travelling into Leeds paid

Top:
Armley Moor in 1987. All has long since been swept away, and two 'Pacer' DMUs pass the site with Leeds and Bradford trains on 21 September. *S. R. Batty*

Left:
Altofts was the junction of the Y&NMR line from York with the Leeds-Derby line of the NMR. Class 37 No 37077 *British Steel Shelton* passes the junction with a train of oil tanks on 25 January 1986. *S. R. Batty*

only 5d! Passengers for Bradford often used a Halifax train to Laister Dyke, where a change could be made for a second train into Adolphus Street, but this depended upon the unwary traveller being able to hear the porter's miserable shouting at Laister Dyke, otherwise he would be quickly whisked away towards Bowling and Low Moor stations.

Main Lines to Leeds

Leeds was favoured as a prime target for some of the earliest trunk route main lines proposed during the first 'Railway Mania' in the hectic years of 1835-36. The two most important were the NMR and the M&LR. Much has already been said about the M&LR in previous chapters, but the NMR was the first trunk route opened to Leeds and it gave access to London via the towns and cities of the Midlands as well as giving a roundabout access to Sheffield via Rotherham. A significant connection was built at Altofts, near Normanton, which gave access to York and, eventually, Newcastle and Edinburgh. Construction of the NMR was started at Clay Cross tunnel, near Chesterfield, in February 1837 and should have seen the railway reach Leeds by early 1840 for an estimated expenditure of £1.25 million, but delays at the Leeds end due

to arguments over land purchase from the Aire & Calder Navigation Co caused some delay and a final expenditure of £3 million. The NMR's Leeds station was at first intended to have been built on a site adjacent to Leeds Bridge, but the canal interests prevented this and the NMR had to build their station in Hunslet Lane, some way out of the town centre and placed amidst the heavy engineering industry which was growing up rapidly in the township of Hunslet. This station became unique in the history of Leeds railway stations for attracting considerable acclaim at its opening, being of generous proportions and handsome appearance. It was built by T. Jackson, a London builder who had also built Derby station, and comprised a frontage of 179ft width and 28ft 6in depth, with a six-track train shed which was 267ft long and 113ft 6in wide. A central arcade, 6ft wide, was provided within the two-storey building. The only other major civil engineering feature in the locality was the six-arch viaduct, built across the river and the canal at Altofts by Hugh McIntosh, but the wide, curving sweeps of the line and tall embankments and wide cuttings captured the imagination of the early railway travellers to an extent only equalled by some of Brunel's works between London and Bristol.

The directors' train passed along the line on

Above left:
A St Pancras-Bradford express passes Stourton behind a BR/Sulzer 'Peak' as '8F' 2-8-0 No 48721 takes a breather from shunting duties. *E. Treacy*

Above:
The spur between Engine Shed and Whitehall junctions allowed some traffic to bypass Leeds (City) station. Class '8F' 2-8-0 No 48202 with a Carlisle freight runs alongside Class 'D49/2' 4-4-0 No 62775 *The Tynedale* on the approach to the junction. *E. Treacy*

30 June and, although the line was to be opened to the public on the next day, the carriage of heavy goods traffic was not, at that time, expected to be undertaken just yet — construction was still to be completed before the full passenger and goods timetables could be put into service. London was to be reached within 9½-11hr of leaving Leeds right from the start of the public service, and this one feature was the greatest improvement in travel facilities ever seen by the people of Leeds. The abundance of cheap local travel and excursion trains for the vast majority of the population was only just around the corner but, in 1840, the ability to travel from Leeds to London in less than a day was a miraculous improvement on the times taken by the stagecoaches which

What appears to be a very old half-mile post, still in use today as a stepping-stone alongside the Calder Valley main line. *S. R. Batty*

had plied the route for generations past. The significance of these events was not lost on the directors, who sat down to a very jolly and excited lunch with 400 guests at the Music Hall in Albion Street afterwards.

On the great day itself, a train of 34 first and second-class coaches carrying between 500 and 600 passengers left Hunslet Lane at 08.00 amidst cheering crowds. A 'good rattling pace' (to quote a journalist of the day) was set to Oulton, reached at 08.15, and was followed by a water stop at Methley. The train reached Oakenshaw (at that time the station for Wakefield) at 09.05, where more carriages were attached from the Y&NMR for the journey on to Derby via Cudworth and Masborough (the Y&NMR opened simultaneously through from York to Altofts Junction). After arrival at Derby at 13.10, the passengers devoured a cold lunch before the return departure at 14.30. A brisker run home followed and the 18.55 arrival was followed by another dinner at the Music Hall.

The NMR's origins and Act of Parliament lay in the 1835-36 'Railway Mania', and the rapid construction and promotion of railways generally in this period saw the line in use within five years of receiving its Act. The M&LR had a much longer gestation period due to the scheme being a much older one which came up against some powerful opposition from the canal interests, as mentioned previously. Plans laid in 1824 were quickly defeated, but during the following year George Stephenson and James Walker surveyed a line along the Calder Valley as far as Brighouse, and then towards Low Moor and Pudsey where the first proposed Leeds-Bradford 'Short line' would be joined for the remainder of the journey to Leeds. This would certainly have been a good route to follow, but the combined power of three canal companies — the Aire & Calder, the Calder & Hebble and the Rochdale — quashed the idea in October 1831. It was not until July 1836 that the M&LR finally received their Act after surveying further along the Calder Valley to reach Leeds by a rather roundabout route via Mirfield, Horbury and Normanton which avoided Halifax, Dewsbury and Bradford but passed through a total population of 420,000 directly on the route and a further 900,000 within the immediate vicinity. George Stephenson had to relax his strict ideas regarding ruling gradients and his more usual

Facing page, top:
The diverted Sunday 10.40 Liverpool-York leaves Elland tunnel on 17 October 1982 behind 'Peak' No 45129.
J. S. Whiteley

Facing page, bottom:
The M&LR main line joined that of the NMR at Goose Hill Junction, Normanton, for the remainder of the journey to Leeds. Class 40 No 40056 hauls a tank train from Lancashire past milepost 50 at Locke's Siding on the approach to Goose Hill Junction on 23 September 1981.
L. A. Nixon

Left:
A Class 47 takes the Calder Valley route at the now abolished Goose Hill Junction with a tank train in February 1988. *S. R. Batty*

figure of 1 in 330 was eased to 1 in 160 to account for the climb to the 2,885yd Summit tunnel near Todmorden. No less than 11 tunnels and 22 viaducts were to be constructed, and the stations were to be built in the style of 'Elizabethan villas'. This feature caused some grumblings about extravagance among the shareholders, but the directors believed that all the materials required would be readily found along the route and no great expense would be required; indeed they went so far as to say that these stations would cost less than those built by other railways. One commentator of the day was rash enough to say that, '. . . it is quite impossible that any line can ever be made to compete with it . . .' and

went on to say that the resulting monopoly should be of a magnitude and power equal to or greater than that exercised by the Aire & Calder Navigation.

Even before work started in August 1837 the company was compelled to go back to Parliament with another Bill to amend the original Act. Having realised just what they had taken on, the M&LR sought powers to raise more money and to alter the route slightly in order to save on building costs (by easing gradients and curvature), and an amendment to the original Act was made in May 1837. Construction went ahead and the first section was opened from Manchester to Littleborough on 4 July 1839, followed by

Right:
Class 47 No 47312 passes Goose Hill Junction with empty newspaper vans for Manchester on 3 August 1986. *S. R. Batty*

Below:
Standard Class '5' 4-6-0 No 73039 approaches Morley tunnel with the 09.30 (SO) Manchester-Newcastle on 8 July 1967. *M. Mitchell*

Above right:
Stanier Class '5' No 45232 and 'Jubilee' No 45737 *Atlas* forge past Ward's Siding, west of Farnley Junction, with a York-Manchester ecs train on 16 August 1962. *M. Mitchell*

Hebden Bridge-Normanton on 5 October 1840 and Summit-Hebden Bridge on 31 December 1840. The great tunnel at Summit, which was the longest railway tunnel in the world for three months after opening until Brunel's Box tunnel was opened, was not completed until the spring of 1841 and the entire line was opened for public use on Monday 1 March 1841. For a major railway which was to form the bulk of the Liverpool-Hull scheme, the actual opening was a very modest affair. A two-coach train conveyed the Manchester directors and both engineers, Stephenson and Gooch, from Manchester (Oldham Road) station at 09.20 eastwards at an average speed of 30mph. Bands played at Summit and at

Ossett, and the small train went as far as Normanton before reversing to Wakefield for a lunch in the goods shed. Parliament had not approved the M&LR plan of 1836 to reach Leeds by building a duplicate line alongside that of the (then) planned NMR, and had decided that they should have running powers over the NMR from Normanton to Hunslet Lane stations. This was presumably the reason why the directors reversed back to Wakefield, and probably also the first sign of discontent felt by those the M&LR was supposed to serve in Yorkshire — it was, after all, the Manchester & *Leeds* Railway, not the Manchester & Wakefield or Manchester & Normanton! The small party arrived back in Manchester at

Class 47 No 47418 roars away from Dewsbury with the 09.03 Liverpool-Newcastle on 2 July 1987. *S. R. Batty*

Above:
Looking in the opposite direction to the previous picture, No 47422 leaves Batley and hauls the 08.25 Newcastle-Liverpool off the Union Mill viaduct on 2 July 1987. *S. R. Batty*

Above right:
A Leeds-bound parcels train crosses the viaduct towards Batley on 29 September 1962. The right-hand tracks are part of the GNR Tingley-Batley-Wakefield route, and the full extent of the final LNWR/GNR station area can be seen in the background. *D. I. Wood*

Right:
Class '5' 4-6-0 No 44934 climbs the 1 in 120 past Farnley Junction MPD with a Leeds-Manchester local (via Dewsbury) in the late 1950s. *K. Field*

16.45, the Leeds directors having taken no part in the day's events. Regular passenger and goods traffic started in full on the same day (with the directors' train sandwiched in between), and the passenger timetable was as outlined below.

06.30 Brighouse-Manchester	06.15 Sowerby Bridge-Leeds
Manchester-Leeds trains departing at 06.30, 08.00, 08.30, 10.30, 11.30, 13.00, 16.00, 18.30	Leeds-Manchester trains departing at 06.45, 08.00, 09.00, 10.30, 12.30, 14.15, 16.00, 18.30
19.30 Manchester-Brighouse	19.30 Leeds-Sowerby Bridge

The canal companies suffered right from the start of M&LR services getting underway. Initially the M&LR used a fleet of steamers to take goods from Manchester on to Liverpool and this scuppered the Leeds & Liverpool Canal Co. The Leeds directors of the M&LR were determined to have a through route from Liverpool to Hull and, in December ˙1843, agreement was reached with the H&SR to get trains through to Hull. In May 1844 the M&LR opened a joint station in Manchester with the L&MR at Hunts Bank and through railway travel from Liverpool to Hull became a reality, 20 years after first being visualised.

The last years of the 1840s saw the completion of two important trunk routes into Leeds. These were the Leeds-Dewsbury-Mirfield route, opened by the LNWR on 18 September 1848, and the Leeds & Thirsk Railway (L&TR) which gave access to Harrogate, Thirsk and the northeast from 9 July 1849. Today these two routes demonstrate clearly how former main lines can be affected in different ways by the passage of time and changing circumstances. The ex-LNWR line continues in use as a busy passenger-carrying route, gradually improved over the years such that it survives today in much the same form as it has operated over the past 60 years or so. Rationalisation and modernisation, to use two overworked expressions, have certainly made themselves felt — small stations and goods yards have long since disappeared — but the route remains well used and has an established future. The ex-L&TR serves only Harrogate, Knaresborough and now York, and the through expresses to the northeast dis-

appeared in the mid-1960s. Beyond Harrogate nothing remains of this important main line, just as very little trace is left of the triangular junction at Arthington built to give access to Otley and Ilkley.

The LD&MR was incorporated on 30 June 1845 and was essentially a locally-sponsored company formed to build part of a much better route from Leeds to Manchester than that offered by the M&LR. A line was to be built to a point at Heaton Lodge, beyond Mirfield, where a junction would be made with the H&MR's line which was to pass through Huddersfield, climb to a tunnel at Standedge and then descend to Manchester via Stalybridge. The H&MR was incorporated on 21 July 1845 and the two companies lost no time in getting work under way. Just over a year later the M&LR entered the scene by way of taking over the Huddersfield & Sheffield Junction Railway (H&SJR), whose line was to run from Huddersfield to Penistone on the Sheffield, Ashton-under-Lyne & Manchester Railway. The M&LR had to do something to make sure they could have access to Huddersfield to get to their latest acquisition from other parts of their system, and duly made moves for a take-over of the two companies. However, the LD&MR and H&MR priced themselves above the M&LR's means, but a takeover by the LNWR quickly followed. The LNWR thus penetrated the West Riding with a brand-new main line, which was connected to the heart of their empire in Manchester, and in so doing reduced the length of journey from Leeds to Manchester from 61 miles via Normanton to 41 miles via Huddersfield. To avoid building a duplicate main line from Thornhill to Heaton Lodge the LNWR negotiated running powers over the LYR (as the M&LR had become) between these points, in return granting the use of their Heaton Lodge-Huddersfield section to the LYR. More co-operation followed with the LNWR being allowed to use LYR metals in Manchester and, more importantly, with the LYR then sending most of their Leeds and Manchester trains over the new route via Dewsbury.

A considerable amount of civil engineering was necessary on the LD&MR line, the heaviest being the 3,370yd tunnel at Morley. Thomas Grainger was the engineer responsible for building the 10½-mile railway and his principal contractors were J. & R. Crawshaw, Nowell & Hattersley, and Shaw's. Stations were built at Churwell, Morley, Batley and Dewsbury and bridges and viaducts at Leeds and Dewsbury. Dewsbury's Union Mill viaduct comprised 18 arches of 30ft span and the River

Calder was crossed by a twin-arched iron bridge with each span measuring 100ft. The canal was crossed by a single span of similar design, and the WRUR's Dewsbury branch passed between the two. Leeds viaduct, taking the railway from what was to become Central station to a point just beyond the L&BR line, was particularly impressive. A 35ft girder bridge crossed Lower Queen Street, and was followed by 33 stone arches of 30ft span and 20 arches of 35ft span, one of 105ft over the River Aire, another of 70ft over the Leeds & Liverpool Canal and finally a 70ft span girder bridge over the Leeds & Bradford line of the MR. The keystone was laid during January 1848 at a ceremony attended by Grainger, Shaw and George Thompson, who had been engaged to build this particular feature of the new line. Commercial success was felt to be a foregone conclusion for the LD&MR, due to the much better route offered to Manchester and to the booming trade of the heavy woollen district which was centred on Dewsbury. Populations of 152,000 and 13,000 were to be found at Leeds and Dewsbury respectively, with 1,200 at Churwell, 5,000 at Morley, 4,800 at Batley and almost 60,000 in the nearby Spen Valley. Dewsbury's trade was that of buying wool remnants and reconstituting them into a coarse, loosely-woven cloth known as shoddy or, if it was felted, mungo. The LNWR was to bring prosperity to the town's rag merchants.

After inspection by Capt Simmonds on 20 July 1848 the line was declared to be open to the public from 1 August. The official opening ceremonies took place on 31 July, starting with a train formed of '. . . a powerful engine and eight carriages principally of the first class . . .' which left Leeds station at 13.00, 1hr after the intended departure time (the station was known in later years as Leeds Central, but in July 1848 it was an incomplete terminus which was at the centre of much wrangling and argument amongst the companies who had supposedly agreed to build it nearly two years previously. For the LD&MR opening a quickly-remodelled warehouse, formerly used by Schunk & Co, was pressed into service). The first train reached the junction with the LYR line at Thornhill in 35min and took a further 20min to reach Huddersfield. After lunch the party (which included Grainger, the Chief Engineer, Rhodes, the head of the LD&MR locomotive department, and Fenton of the Leeds foundry, Fenton, Murray & Jackson) returned to Leeds after stopping at Dewsbury to meet passengers off two further trains which had travelled from Leeds. More trains ran later in the day, but the last two did not venture further than the LYR junction as there was uncertainty as to whether or not arrangements had in fact been made for these trains to go forward to Huddersfield. Consequently the passengers had no refreshment, but some enterprising platform sellers then appeared and quickly sold out their stocks amongst the ravenous travellers. Some of the ladies on the trains had to face further pangs of hunger, along with some embarrassment, later in the day when the celebration dinner was held for 350 guests at the Music Hall in Leeds. Someone had decided this should be a men-only event, but had not apparently informed those responsible for selling the tickets — consequently many ladies with tickets were turned away, and the company was roundly condemned in the press for this incident (and several others on the same day) and for generally displaying a 'want of gallantry' towards the offended ladies.

Below:
The site of Farnley Junction MPD in 1985. Class 47 No 47609 *Fire Fly* passes with the 13.55 Scarborough-Liverpool on 18 September 1985. Lineside undergrowth almost touches the train, and the former New Line and MPD site are completely engulfed by vegetation. *S. R. Batty*

Right:
The 11.20 Newcastle-Liverpool leaves Morley tunnel and approaches Batley behind Class 47 No 47555 *The Commonwealth Spirit* on 12 June 1985. *S. R. Batty*

Despite being part of the LNWR (or perhaps because of it) the LD&MR does not appear to have been on very good terms with the parent company. Perhaps as a last gesture of independence, no LNWR directors were invited to the opening ceremony. The LNWR replied by stating quite simply that it did not recognise the line as being opened! The LD&MR then insisted that full recognition must be given from 7 August, and this act of insolence towards the 'Premier Line' resulted in the despatch of Capt Mark Huish to Leeds to sort matters out. Huish was the LNWR General Manager, and his visit resulted in an 'official' opening ceremony taking place on 18 September. Thus, although the LD&MR was ceremonially opened to Huddersfield on 31 July, the arguments which followed delayed the full public opening by nearly seven weeks beyond that date. A total of 11 trains ran daily each way, with four on Sundays, the expresses taking 50min for the journey. A slight accident occurred on 21 September when the 14.00 train from Huddersfield collided with the buffers at Leeds station. As has already been mentioned in connection with the LBHJR, arriving trains were coasted into the temporary station under the control of a brakeman. This operation was duly performed with the Huddersfield train, but the 'breaks' (to quote the press report of the incident) either failed or were incorrectly controlled, resulting in a collision. Fortunately very little injury took place, and no railway rolling stock was damaged.

The L&TR was conceived as a measure to connect Leeds with Harrogate and to break Hudson's monopoly of traffic to the northeast, which ran via the Y&NMR through Methley and York. A prospectus was issued in May 1844 and the Parliamentary Act was received on 21 July 1845. The connections on to the L&BR main line were made in Leeds, at Armley Junction and Wortley Junction, and a terminus was at first provided in temporary accommodation on Wellington Street, shared with the LD&MR. Construction work started on 20 October 1845 and proceeded rapidly despite some massive civil engineering works. The greatest of these was Bramhope tunnel, 3,671yd of waterlogged excavation which killed many men and delayed the opening through to Ripon until 9 July 1849, when the line was officially opened and three trains carried 2,000 shareholders along the route. Earlier openings had seen the L&TR opened through from Thirsk to Weeton, south of

Below:

Class 40 No 40074 passes Batley station with the 08.10 Liverpool-Newcastle on 27 November 1978. *G. W. Morrison*

Above:
Class '5' 4-6-0 No 44828 takes empty stock out of Leeds (Central) over the graceful stone bridge across the River Aire on 19 July 1966.
V. L. Murphy

Left:
This shell of a former wagon lift is all that remains of the goods yards which once existed around Leeds (Central) station. *S. R. Batty*

Harrogate, by 13 September 1848, and the opening of the last section from Leeds to Weeton excited very little comment in the contemporary press.

Leeds Central Station

Today's remains of this fascinating terminus are very few indeed, and a trained eye and long memory are needed in order to pick out what few reminders are left. Built on an elevated site on the south side of Wellington Street about 300yd west of City Square, the station was closed to passengers from 1 May 1967 and the site was soon cleared and levelled to make way for new development. The Royal Mail building now stands where the station buildings once stood (but built from street level, unlike the station), and whereas Central station was credited with very little architectural merit, the new building has absolutely none whatsoever and forms just another concrete blot amidst the modern Leeds landscape. The embankment which once carried the approach lines from Copley Hill and Gelderd Junction has also been completely removed and replaced by a collection of shops, warehouses and industrial premises unequalled within many a mile for their liverish colours and general ghastliness of appearance. Two original features are prominent within the area — a stone-built wagon lift which once operated between the high and low-level goods yards, and the viaduct across the river and canal. The former Great Northern Hotel, renamed The Wellesley, still survives as a solitary monument to the station which once stood alongside, fronting Wellington Street. Central station was small, dark and rather dingy, but for sheer railway atmosphere — perhaps 'feel' is a better term — it was unequalled in the West Riding. Perhaps the rich history of its origins and evolution left an indelible stamp which lasted throughout its life of some 113 years.

In the early 1840s four railway companies were building lines to Leeds which would all need a station somewhere near the city centre. These were the LD&MR, the L&TR, the WRUR and, ultimately, the GNR. The L&BR had already settled on a site at Leeds (Wellington), and this came into use on 1 July 1846 as already described. The first of several plans for a 'central' station was drawn up in November 1844 by the LD&MR and L&TR, who actually proposed separate but adjoining stations on Wellington Street. Later in the same month common sense seems to have prevailed when the LD&MR, L&TR, the L&WRJ and the London & York (soon to become the GNR) presented plans for a jointly-owned station on the same site. The London & York Railway (L&YR) and the L&WRJR were hopeful of gaining their own Acts of incorporation during 1845, but these hopes were premature and both were refused, thus weakening the joint plan severely. On top of this the L&TR had cold feet and delayed giving any support to the idea until the outcome of the M&LR's proposed takeover of the L&BR was resolved. The Thirsk company ran on to the L&BR line at Armley and they perhaps saw a chance to get into Wellington station directly if the takeover went ahead. Wellington station was easily accessible for the L&TR and gave good connections to the MR and M&LR systems, whereas the proposed Central station was still an unknown quantity. However, the merger fell through, the L&BR

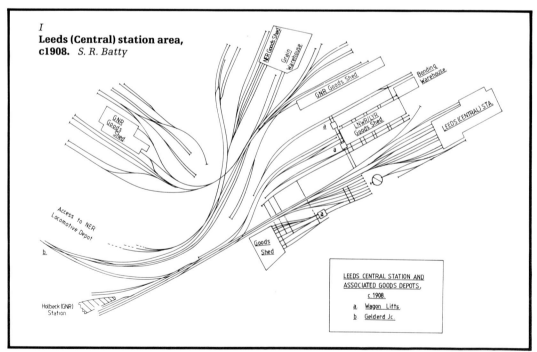

I
Leeds (Central) station area, c1908. *S. R. Batty*

LEEDS CENTRAL STATION AND
ASSOCIATED GOODS DEPOTS,
c.1908
a   Wagon Lifts
b   Gelderd Jc

Above:
A six-car DMU formation from Harrogate climbs up the steep connection from Gelderd Junction to Central station on 10 September 1966. The L&BR tracks are in the foreground, and the access to the GNR/NER goods depots can be seen below the DMU. *D. Butterfield*

went to the MR, and the Thirsk company threw in their lot with the LD&MR again and accepted their part in the Central station proposals. The L&TR was one of Hudson's enemies, and his MR could not be expected to offer access to and accommodation at Wellington station.

The LD&MR and L&TR were the survivors of the original plan of November 1844, and one year later these two partners planned a smaller venture on the same site, but history is unclear as to whether this idea even saw the light of day in paper form. In 1846 the WRUR and the L&YR received their Acts and the new companies immediately revived their interest in access to Leeds. The WRUR was a protégé of the M&LR, and the L&YR scheme was by then known as the GNR. Although the GNR main

line from London to York via Peterborough, Grantham and Doncaster was passed by Parliament, the planned branch from Doncaster to Wakefield and Leeds was rejected in spite of much argument and debate by Edmund Denison, the GNR chairman. Denison was determined to get the GNR entrenched in the West Riding and he did not let this setback reduce his efforts in finding a station for the railway he was sure would one day reach Leeds.

These four companies again made plans for a joint station, and in late 1846 the proposed Central station was to be built near Park Row for a cost of around £500,000. This large sum presumably included the building of a lengthy viaduct to take the LD&MR across Wellington Street to the new terminus. The L&TR would reach the station via a steep spur built up from the L&BR line. However, the L&TR ran into financial difficulty in 1847 and the station proposals were delayed as a result. Two other significant events of that year also had effects on Central station. The first was the LNWR takeover of the LD&MR from 9 July, which meant that the Central station proposals were

now under the scrutiny of an extremely powerful railway company which was just as anxious to get to Leeds as was the GNR. The second development concerned the GNR itself, which in 1847 finally gained access to Leeds by using running powers over the Midland from Methley. During the 1846 session the Wakefield, Pontefract & Goole Railway (WP&GR) had received an Act for a line from Askern to Methley, via Pontefract, which started at an end-on junction with the GNR at Askern. The GNR could now see their way to Leeds, if only the MR could be persuaded to grant running powers from Methley to Leeds. To force the issue the GNR proposed building short branches from the WP&GR at Pontefract to Wakefield and to Leeds. The MR retaliated with a proposal for a cut-off line from Chevet to Rothwell, but Parliament preferred the GNR plan. This, however, was rejected purely on a technicality — but the MR realised that nothing could now keep the GNR out of Leeds, and promptly offered running powers from Methley towards Leeds, but not into Welling-

ton station. The MR saw that any haggling would have been pointless and expensive to all concerned, and also probably realised that the GNR would eventually have its own independent access from Doncaster to Leeds, from whence the running powers would be abandoned to all practical purposes. The agreement took legal effect from October 1847, by which time also the WP&GR had been fully taken over by the L&YR, itself the successor to the M&LR.

A cheaper version of Central station was proposed, in 1848, costing £258,000 and having separate arrival and departure platforms for each of the four companies, ie the L&TR, LNWR, GNR and LYR (the LYR had absorbed the West Riding Union by this time). This cheaper structure would still have reached across Wellington Street to Infirmary Street, and no progress was made with actual construction. The LD&MR opening was rapidly approaching, but nothing had been done to provide a terminal station at the Leeds end of the line, and the aforementioned warehouse was quickly acquired and refitted for railway use in time for the opening of the line in July. More uncertainty followed and yet another cost-cutting exercise was undertaken in early 1849 which led to the construction of Central station as finally built. The £258,000

Below:
Leeds (Central) in the 1950s — 'N1' 0-6-2T No 69447 awaits departure with a local train.
K. Field

version was reduced in cost to between £60-70,000, largely by keeping the station to the south of Wellington Street and by greatly reducing the number of platforms to be built. A high-level station, on the lines of the LD&MR proposal, was to be built and low-level goods space was to be provided for the GNR and L&TR companies. Space at the high-level passenger station was reduced when the LYR came along and insisted on having a goods depot included for their use, probably because the MR was keen to get them out of the Hunslet Lane depot. At this time the GNR became rather unhappy with the way events were turning at Central station and eventually threatened to withdraw from the idea. The LYR demand was seen as an LNWR-inspired plot to make life difficult for the GNR (along the lines of the unofficial Euston Square Confederacy), and the GNR access to the planned station was awkward to say the least. This involved running into Leeds along the Midland line through to Armley and then reversing from Gelderd Junction up to the high-level Central station. To overcome this the GNR planned to build a direct line to a low-level station from a point just before today's Whitehall Junction, which would have crossed the L&BR and LD&MR lines before reaching a small station amidst the GNR and

L&TR goods depots. Nothing came of this plan, and the GNR appears to have cooled off and decided to stick to their original plans.

Construction started early in 1849 (the Leeds Central Station Act was passed on 22 July 1848), but the L&TR had to share temporary accommodation with the LD&MR at their opening on 9 July of that year.

The first LNWR train to run through from Manchester via Huddersfield and Dewsbury also had to use these facilities when they commenced running from 1 August. Trouble brewed in the following year when arguments over land allocation stopped all work and the L&TR and LNWR promptly departed for Wellington station. The L&TR went ahead with their low-level goods depot, and the GNR bought running powers over these lines to ensure access to their depot built alongside. They also built a temporary passenger station there and brought it into use from May 1850, vacating the Central station proper. Passengers on the L&TR were diverted to Wellington

Below:
Class 'J50' No 68988 stands at the buffer stops on station pilot duty on 11 January 1959.
M. Mitchell

station from the same month and in the following October the LNWR opened the Copley Hill-Whitehall Junction connection and also defected to Wellington. Consequently only the LYR was left in Central station, sending Manchester trains in from the Dewsbury route as agreed at the opening of the LD&M line in 1849.

By this time the railway users of Leeds were well and truly fed up with temporary stations, diversions, delays and general confusion over the railway termini of their city. One single central station was called for, and the general preference was for the Wellington station to fill this need. With only the LYR left using the incomplete Central station this preference was just about met during 1850 (even some of the LYR traffic was occasionally sent to Wellington via the new LNWR line). Nevertheless, the joint effort went ahead and in June 1851 became the responsibility of the LNWR, LYR and L&TR. The GNR remained bottled up in their low-level cupboard, perhaps sulking

more than a little at their bad management which had landed them in a very difficult position. Having gone to a great deal of trouble to get themselves into Leeds, they had allowed themselves to become jammed in amongst a cramped collection of goods sheds, totally unsuitable for passenger traffic and hopelessly inadequate for any future main line developments. Salvation came with the incorporation of the LBHJR in 1852 (previously described), and with the formation in 1854 of the Bradford, Wakefield & Leeds Railway (to be described later). These lines were to meet at Wortley and then terminate in Central station, and this feature was quickly seized upon by the GNR as a means of finally gaining access to the high-level Central terminus. Powers were gained for the new lines to be worked by the GNR in the new Companies' Acts, and the GNR then became the fourth partner in the venture alongside the LNWR, LYR and L&TR. The Bradford, Wakefield & Leeds (BW&LR) was to give a direct line to Wakefield, so ridding the GNR of any future dependence on the MR for access from Methley. Yet more rebuilding followed in 1855 after an accident took place at the station (which had not progressed much beyond the arguments over land allocation of five years previously), and the finished station

Below:

A classic departure from Central — King's Cross 'V2' 2-6-2 No 60903 gets underway with the 15.15 London express on 20 June 1950. *H. Weston*

was finally opened in 1857, the year in which the BW&LR was opened. Thirteen years had passed since Central station was first mooted, and time has certainly told on the original proposers — the LD&MR (or LNWR) and L&TR (by then part of the North Eastern Railway) had settled in at Wellington, the WRUR had long since failed, the LYR (previously the M&LR) maintained a token presence bolstered by their running powers over the GNR-backed LBHJR line, and the GNR itself, once the most junior partner, became the principal operator of the new station. The actual 'opening' date of the station will always be an impossible moment to pinpoint due to the complicated sequence of events leading to the eventual completion of the station. The year of 1857, which saw the building completed, cannot be

Above:

The up 'Yorkshire Pullman' leaves Central station behind Class 'A1' 4-6-2 No 60117 *Bois Roussel* deputising for a failed diesel on 13 April 1964. *E. Treacy*

specified as an opening date as trains had been using the station since 1850 in some manner or other. But the actual fabric of the terminus barely existed at all until 1855, although the GNR was established in the high-level platforms by then. Perhaps it would be more accurate to say that the station was eventually built over the 13 years from 1844, despite the lack of any co-ordination amongst those companies who were anxious, at various times, for its urgent completion.

3 Great Northern Expansion

The GNR Reaches Leeds

The penetration of the GNR into Leeds was of course the beginning of this company's long and colourful association with the West Riding of Yorkshire. GNR services became an integral part of railway life in Leeds and Bradford, and the network of suburban services built up by the company in the years to 1914 was second to none for smart running and for the amount of hilly, twisting route mileage which demanded the best from men and machines. Road traffic saw the end of all this, but the GNR's express passenger connections along their main line to King's Cross became famous throughout the LNER years, and lived on to develop into today's electrified ECML service. The GNR service to Leeds and Bradford has always been in the limelight of railway operation, and the GNR's first entry to Leeds was certainly a newsworthy event in 1849. Methley is a small village, close by the former NMR main line between Leeds and

Below:
Gildersome GNR station in July 1965, just over a year after closure to passengers. *M. Mitchell*

Normanton, and no doubt was even smaller when the events of 140 years ago took place.

As described earlier, the GNR's original Bill of 1846 for a London and York Railway with branches to Wakefield and Leeds was rejected on a technicality by Parliament. The same session saw approval given to the WP&GR branch from Askern to Methley, which gave the GNR a chance to reach Leeds quickly from their main line north of Doncaster. Running powers were granted to Methley on 1 May 1847, over 2½ years before the Pontefract-Methley line was completed, and there remained only the problem for the GNR of getting from Methley to Leeds. Although the MR detested the idea of having the GNR as a competitor — Hudson had, it will be remembered, proposed his own new lines as alternatives to the GNR Leeds and Wakefield branches — Hudson realised that Parliament favoured the GNR branches and that opposition was useless. Running powers from Methley to Leeds were granted on 16 October 1847, long before any actual running could be done by the GNR. The WP&GR was taken over by the LYR in July 1847, the main line from Wakefield to Goole via Pontefract and

Knottingley was opened on 1 April 1848 and the branch from Knottingley to Askern followed on 6 June. The GNR branch from here to the main line at Arksey Junction opened the next day, but the vital LYR branch from Pontefract up to Methley was not due for completion until late the following year. During this long period the MR began to feel uneasy about having the GNR running in competition to Leeds and they were certainly not pleased at allowing the use of their main line from Methley into Leeds. One may ask, why then did the Midland grant running powers in the first place? The answer lies with Hudson, who undoubtedly realised that the GNR would, sooner or later, build their own line anyway and that such powers would lapse before too long. Had the MR not agreed, the GNR would have built their Leeds branch sooner rather than later, but by 1849 Hudson had vanished in disgrace from the railway scene, leaving the MR free to make life rather

difficult for the GNR. As the opening of the Pontefract-Methley line drew near in the late summer of 1849, the MR decided that it did not want to see the GNR have the lion's share of the lucrative traffic generated by the St Leger race meeting at Doncaster during September. The GN would reach Doncaster from Leeds via Pontefract as well as from the south via their own main line, but the best the MR could

Below:
Stanier 'Black Five' No 45206 approaches Gildersome West on 10 August 1960 with a Bradford-King's Cross train. *M. Mitchell*

Bottom:
On the same day, 'B1' 4-6-0 No 61387 passes Tingley with a Bradford-Cleethorpes train. The route to Gildersome and Wakefield was rich in minerals during the 1850s, and today the area is riddled with old mine workings. *M. Mitchell*

Above:
'B1' 4-6-0 No 61034 *Chiru* climbs past Cutlers Junction towards Broad Lane Junction and Dudley Hill with the 15.09 Bradford-King's Cross on 3 August 1964. *M. Mitchell*

Below:
The short spur between Wortley West and South Junctions provided a direct route from Bradford to Wakefield by avoiding reversal at Leeds (Central). Class '4MT' 2-6-4T No 42650 clears the West Junction with a King's Cross-Wakefield-Bradford train on 20 August 1966. *L. A. Nixon*

Wortley South Junction was removed during 1985, leading to legal action against BR by various parties. 'Peak' No 45029 passes the site on 22 June 1987 with a Peak Forest-Leeds (Balm Road) stone train, one of the few freight duties over this route to Wakefield. *S. R. Batty*

manage was to arrange to send some traffic to Doncaster via Swinton. The last straw came when the Swinton route was completely blocked by a landslip which could not be cleared in time to let the MR operate any St Ledger traffic at all, and the MR then demanded that the GNR should never construct their own line into Leeds! Until the assurance was given, the MR would charge extortionate tolls from all GNR passengers using the Leeds-Methley section. Naturally the GNR would not agree to this blackmail and the intended opening of the Pontefract-Methley branch on 3 September had to be postponed until the argument was resolved. This was referred to in the local press, rather politely in view of the background skulduggery, as 'some misunderstanding between the Midland Company and the directors of the other line'.

The 'other line' was, of course, the LYR, and quite how their directors felt about the MR's interference over agreed running powers granted to the GNR in 1847, and also about the delay caused to the opening of their own branch line, can perhaps be well imagined. Events reached a peak with the 'Methley Incident' which took place during the week of 4-11 September (exact dates vary according to sources). To prevent the passage of any GNR trains the MR officers took the simple, effective and highly dangerous step of removing the points at Methley Junction. Fortunately the GNR at Doncaster realised that something was happening along the line and sent a light engine and crew ahead of the first trains to make sure the way was clear. A calamity, possibly with loss of life, was avoided and strong protests from the GNR and LYR followed. Meanwhile the GNR made diversionary arrangements for the Leeds-Doncaster St Leger traffic whilst legal action was threatened against the MR. The race specials ran from 12 September, but it appears that these GN trains started from Wakefield Kirkgate station to Doncaster via Featherstone, Pontefract, Knottingley and Askern with the LYR running a connecting Leeds-Wakefield service via Normanton. The GNR Peterborough-Doncaster-Leeds service was started during this week, but it was not until 1 October that the Methley branch was brought into use, as originally intended. The GNR trains at this time travelled along the L&BR for a short distance before reversing into the LD&MR/L&TR joint station in Wellington Street.

Further Lines — Leeds, Wakefield and Bradford

Any prospective railway traveller of the early 1850s who sought to reach Wakefield from Bradford was faced with the tedious prospect of travelling along the LYR Spen Valley branch

Above:
The 15.42 Doncaster local passes Beeston, on the climb to Ardsley tunnel, behind 'B1' 4-6-0 No 61115 on 16 August 1962. *M. Mitchell*

Top right:
The 10.50 King's Cross-Leeds HST emerges from Ardsley Tunnel on 18 August 1983. *S. R. Batty*

Right:
The 15.08 Bradford-King's Cross leaves the Bradford direct line via Gildersome and joins the ex-BW&LR line from Leeds at Ardsley on 21 August 1965. *M. Mitchell*

Bottom right:
Another view of the 15.42 Doncaster stopper, this time leaving Ardsley on 10 August 1960 behind 'B1' 4-6-0 No 61189 *Sir William Gray*. Today the site consists of just the two main running lines — the station and yards have disappeared without trace. *M. Mitchell*

via Liversedge and Heckmondwike to Mirfield where, after reversal of direction and a long wait, departure was eventually made along the Calder Valley main line. Travellers from Leeds fared better but still had a lengthy journey via Normanton. In 1853 a branch line was proposed by the LBHJR to run from Laisterdyke to the collieries of the Gildersome area, in order to supply fuel primarily to Bradford and Halifax. The Act was passed on 4 August 1853, but moves had already been made towards improving Bradford's links with Wakefield. The BW&LR was under promotion at about the same time and this line's route was to go through Beeston and Ardsley before reaching a new station at Wakefield. The Gildersome branch — essentially a mineral railway which was intended to carry passengers as a sideline — could easily be extended through Morley and Tingley to reach the BW&LR at Ardsley, so providing a much more direct route to Wakefield, and the necessary Act to extend the Gildersome branch was passed on the same day, 10 July 1854, as the BW&LR received their incorporation. The BW&LR was really a line from Wakefield to Wortley, where a double junction gave access to either Bradford or Leeds via the metals of the LBHJR. Powers were incorporated into the Act for the line to be worked by the GNR and this not only eased their access problems at Central station, as previously mentioned, but also gave them a direct route from Wakefield to Bradford (via their two protégé companies, the BW&LR and LBHJR) via Ardsley, Morley and Laisterdyke.

The Gildersome branch may have been conceived as a dead-ended mineral railway, but the GNR soon dramatically changed its future!

Construction of the two railways went ahead but the LBHJR line was delayed by difficulties with the contractor, who abandoned the job after some argument with the company. Smith & Knight took over, under the supervision of John Hawkshaw as engineer, and firstly built the originally proposed branch from Laisterdyke to Five Lane Ends at Gildersome. Four stations (Dudley Hill, Birkenshaw & Tong, Drighlington & Adwalton and Gildersome)

were built along the six-mile length, and the line was inspected by Capt Tolland on 16 August 1856. A directors' train, carying 100 passengers, left Laisterdyke on 19 August for a jaunt along the line and the contemporary description of the scenery encountered is well worth reading. This stated that the line threaded a region of romantic hills and valleys, rich in mineral wealth, and opened up a rich coalfield of vast extent. Mineral traffic was expected to reach 500-700,000 tons per year, and rails of an especially heavy section had been used to cater for the anticipated heavy traffic demands. New collieries were being built alongside the line, with S. Holliday & Co, Holliday Bros and Mason & Asquith, all near Gildersome station, Bower's near Drighlington & Adwalton station, and both Harrison's and Ackroyd's Oakwell Colliery alongside the railway near Whitehall Road at Drighlington. Even more coal traffic was expected when the extension through to Ardsley was built. Passenger trains reached Gildersome from Bradford in 30min, from Leeds in 1hr and from Halifax in just over 1hr, and the public opening took place on Wednesday 20 August. Perhaps the reference to 'romantic hills and valleys' could be viewed as

Below:
A London express gets underway past Wortley South behind 'A4' Pacific No 60006 *Sir Ralph Wedgewood*. *E. Treacy*

Bottom:
A King's Cross-Leeds express drifts past Beeston Junction behind Class 'A1' Pacific No 60139 *Sea Eagle*. Class 'J6' 0-6-0 No 64277 is standing on the remaining line of the Beeston/Tingley flying junction — the trackbed of the lifted Leeds-bound line can be seen to the right of the signal gantry. *E. Treacy*

Right:
**Adwalton Junction
signalbox, 12 July 1964.**
D. Butterfield

Below right:
**Class '4F' 0-6-0 No 44492 and
'B1' 4-6-0 No 61123 haul the
13.59 (SO) Skegness-Bradford
uphill from Batley to meet
the Gildersome line at
Adwalton Junction on
5 August 1961.** *M. Mitchell*

Below:
**Three years later the train
was leaving Skegness at 14.10
and still required double-
heading over the difficult
route via Batley. 'B1' 4-6-0
No 61040 *Roedeer* and '4MT'
2-6-4T No 42142 climb past
the remains of Howden
Clough signalbox on 8 August
1964.** *M. Mitchell*

Facing page, bottom:
**WD 2-8-0 No 90339 hauls a
freight train towards Healey
Mills past Thornhill on
13 October 1962. The 1869-
built line to Heckmondwike
can be seen on the right.**
J. S. Whiteley

Victorian romanticism *par excellence*, but it must be remembered that the urban sprawl of Leeds, Wakefield and Bradford had not begun in 1856, and the areas between would certainly have been extremely rural, perhaps even beyond belief when one views today's land-scape anywhere along the route of the Gildersome branch. The coal mines are long gone and precious little remains to prove that a railway ever existed.

Extension through to Ardsley was finally accomplished in October 1857, the delays being largely due to problems in building the BW&LR line (there was little point in building on from Gildersome until the Wakefield line was completed). A tunnel of 300yd was built at Ardsley, which must have slowed matters down somewhat, but landslips at Middleton and at Wrenthorpe caused the most serious problems. Formal opening took place on Saturday 3 October 1857, when a special train left Leeds at 14.00 and met another at Ardsley from Bradford, the combined total of 120 passengers then proceeding to Wakefield. The celebrations were very low-key, not to say just plain miserable, and after letting off a few detonators at Westgate station (which had been 'altered from a commodious house') the party returned to a late lunch at the Music Hall in Leeds, without any ceremony at Wakefield. Ardsley was the only station between Leeds and Wakefield, but stations were opened at Lofthouse in 1858 and at Beeston in 1860. The main contractor had been Boulton & Young, and 10 wrought iron bridges were supplied by Joseph Butler of Stanningley Ironworks. Sidings were laid in at Beeston for loading coal and iron ore by the Low Moor Co and at Ardsley a branch was to be built to reach Charlesworth's pits at nearby Thorpe. Public

services started on Monday 5 October, some six months after the original completion date due to the landslips which had occurred. A summit was reached at the junction of the LBHJR line with a climb of 1 in 100 being made at either side. Services over the extension to Gildersome commenced from 10 October, with the GNR working through from Wakefield to Leeds from 1 November and through to Bradford via Gildersome from 1 December. The GNR had running powers which allowed them to travel through Westgate station and then descend to the LYR main line at Kirkgate station, before travelling on to Doncaster via Normanton, Knottingley and Askern. Both the LBHJR and BW&LR were fully absorbed by the GNR in 1865, two years after the latter had renamed itself as the West Yorkshire Railway.

Further developments took place in the 1860s to give the GNR more flexibility in working between Bradford and Wakefield. Batley had been rail-served since the opening of the LD&MR line in 1848, and a short branch line was completed through Carlinghow to Birstall in September 1852. Birstall was only a good stone's throw from Bradford and the LNWR tried to build on from here in a scheme of 1861 which was rejected by Parliament. To rub salt in the wound, the LBHJR successfully applied in 1861 to construct a line from Adwalton Junction, on the Ardsley line, to Batley via part of the Birstall branch, following a route very similar to an earlier LNWR proposal of 1859. On the other side of Dewsbury the LNWR had also met with failure in a joint bid (also in 1859) with the LYR to build lines from Thornhill and Dewsbury through Ossett to a junction with the BW&LR, but a BW&LR branch from Wrenthorpe, north of Wakefield, to Ossett was authorised in 1860

Right:
WD 2-8-0 No 90347 stands at Spen Valley Junction as Standard Class '5' 4-6-0 No 73096 passes with a Leeds-Manchester (Exchange) local on 14 March 1957. *L. Metcalfe*

Below right:
The Calder Valley typified — WD 2-8-0 No 90721 plods westwards between Thornhill and Mirfield with a coal train on 13 April 1964. *J. S. Whiteley*

Bottom:
Ivatt 'N1' 0-6-2T No 69434 tackles the gradient from Dewsbury (Central) to Headfield Junction with a Wakefield local train. *K. Field*

Facing page, top:
The remains of the LYR branch to Dewsbury (Market Place) are used today for access to a cement depot. Class 45/0 'Peak' No 45012 rejoins the Calder Valley main line at Dewsbury East Junction on 20 November 1987 with a train for Earles Sidings in the Hope Valley. *S. R. Batty*

Facing page, bottom:
'B1' 4-6-0 No 61161 passes the Shipley and Wakefield lines at Laisterdyke East Junction with the 08.10 for Cleethorpes on 3 July 1965. Quarry Gap sidings are in the foreground. *M. Mitchell*

and allowed to extend into Batley by a further Act in the following year. A joint LNWR/ LBHJR/BW&LR station was originally intended for Batley but the LNWR, who probably felt quite upset at losing completely to the GNR-sponsored companies, withdrew from the agreement and left the two companies to build what became Batley (GNR) station alongside their own establishment. They also cancelled the LBHJR plan to run into the town from Birstall along part of their branch, leaving the former company to try for a second Act to build a new route via Howden Clough and Upper Batley and this was passed in June 1862. The LBHJR line from Adwalton was opened to Upper Batley in August 1863 and through to Batley in November 1864, just one month before the Wrenthorpe line was completed.

Lancashire & Yorkshire Railway Developments

Another development concerned the building of the Heckmondwike-Thornhill spur by the LYR, together with the associated branch into Dewsbury. This was the remains of the abandoned WRUR scheme of 1846, and the lines had been planned but later rejected by the LYR on grounds of cost. By the 1860s, however, demands were being made for a better LYR Bradford-Wakefield service than was provided by the existing Spen Valley/Calder Valley lines, which included reversal at Mirfield. Resurrection of the old WRUR plan was the simplest solution and the necessary Act was passed in June 1861, together with that for a short line from Dewsbury East Junction, on the Calder Valley line, to a station

at Market Place. The branch opened in August 1866, but the Heckmondwike line took nearly three more years to build and was not fully opened until 1 June 1869. Built by a local contractor, Gregson & Alcock of Ravenswharf, the line was 2½ miles long and left the Cleckheaton branch near Heckmondwike before descending to meet the Calder Valley just east of Thornhill station. A 12-arch viaduct was built across the River Calder and Ravensthorpe station was opened during July 1869. Immediate benefits were a 25min reduction in journey time for passengers from Bradford to Dewsbury, Wakefield and Normanton, and a large reduction in congestion at Mirfield which gave some improvement to the LNWR Manchester-Leeds service. Thus the LYR had established themselves, eventually, in Dewsbury and caught the GNR napping at the same time. The GNR responded with plans for a line from Ossett through Dewsbury to Batley, and the first Act was passed in July 1871. Completion took a long time, mainly because of a severe slump in trade during the 1870s, and the first section from Runtlings Lane Junction, Ossett to Dewsbury (GNR) did not open until 9 September 1874. Public announcement of the opening was not made until the day before, but the first day's business was satisfactory. The GNR's Dewsbury station was still being built (on a central site near the Market Place, in an area known as New Wakefield) and temporary platforms and booking offices were provided. Almost six more years passed before the scheme was finished and Batley was reached by the passenger service during April 1880. The original Ossett-Batley line of 1864 was then downgraded, traffic being sent instead via the new stations at Earlsheaton and Batley Carr.

During the 1870s the ever-present dissatisfaction with LYR services, felt by all those who were unfortunate enough to have to rely on them, came to a head. The GNR, seen as the only means of hope and salvation, was being constantly petitioned by the inhabitants of the LYR-dominated Spen Valley to provide alternative services. Having had an appalling reputation for poor service for so long, one might have expected the LYR to have made some serious attempts at improving matters by the dawn of the 1870s. But this was not to be — indeed matters grew steadily worse throughout the decade. Several reasons could be found, principally the development of the LYR as a 'Lancashire' railway, the competitive effect of the LNWR, and booming trade during the early part of the period. The LNWR had only one major route into the West Riding, but they promoted this with such vigour that the LYR were seen to be lagging sadly behind in terms of the services offered. Many hoped that matters would be greatly improved if the LNWR-planned takeover of the LYR (tried in 1872 and 1873, but refused by Parliament) could be achieved, but this longed-for event was 50 years into the future. Goods traffic was steadily clogging the Calder Valley to choking point, as only double-track was provided and the few goods loops were almost permanently occupied by a succession of slow-moving freight trains. The woollen merchants of Dewsbury and the surrounding heavy woollen district craftily managed to supply uniform material to both sides in the Franco-Prussian war of 1870-71, during which period trade flourished and the LYR main line almost ground completely to a halt.

Deputations to Manchester, demanding better services, achieved nothing at all. Caustic comments in the press produced some desperate attempts by the LYR to improve matters. In Bradford, perhaps the centre of dissatisfaction, comment was passed that the trains should be advertised as running 'when circumstances and the goods trains permit'. The LYR tried producing a false timetable which showed the usual late arrival times as the advertised arrival times, producing a bizarre brand of chaos which can hardly be imagined! By 1880 the GNR was well established in the area, and a succession of deputations from the Yorkshire territory of the LYR to King's Cross station led to further developments in the 1880s which gave the GNR further access to the West Riding for relatively little outlay — a trick by now well practised by the Great Northern. From the mid-1870s the GNR had been continually pressed to build further lines to give better services between Halifax and Wakefield, and finally, in 1881, three schemes were suggested. These were:

1 Halifax-Brighouse-Heckmondwike
2 Lightcliffe-Cleckheaton and Heckmondwike-Batley
3 Halifax-Hipperholme-Brighouse-Cleckheaton-Heckmondwike-Batley.

All these schemes would connect with existing LYR/GNR lines on the way to Wakefield, and the deputations urged the GNR to build any of the three and to put up some of the money from their own sources. The GNR hesitated, perhaps seeing the way events were certain to go. In 1886 they had opened their own Doncaster-Wakefield line (taken over, in the usual GNR style, from the West Riding & Grimsby Co) and so had finally rid themselves of any dependence on the LYR and MR companies for access to Leeds from Doncaster. Building another line to Halifax would deepen their penetration from Doncaster even further, and the LYR (and also the Hull & Barnsley Railway) objected to the plan. In 1882 agreement was reached between the GNR and LYR regarding route-sharing, and the new Halifax proposals were dropped. The GNR was granted running powers to use the Calder Valley main line from Wakefield to Halifax and also to use the LYR Spen Valley route to Low Moor, from where they could reach Bradford, Leeds or Halifax via the ex-LBHJR lines. The LYR got a very

good deal indeed, principally the right to use the West Riding & Grimsby (WRG) route of 1866 from Wakefield to Doncaster, but also including running powers over the Ossett-Wakefield and Gildersome lines and the GNR's new Beeston-Batley line which was being started at this time. Two further new stretches of GNR line — which the LYR would also be allowed to use — were agreed also — the Dudley Hill-Low Moor line and the Headfield Junction-Dewsbury Junction connection. The first line merely connected the lines of the two companies together, whilst the second connected from the LYR Dewsbury branch of the GNR Ossett-Dewsbury line, theoretically allowing LYR trains to enter the GNR station. At Low Moor, the LYR agreed to build a south connection allowing trains to run up the Spen Valley and then directly to Halifax, missing out the previous station halt for reversal. All these matters were covered by an Act of Parliament dated 2 August 1883, but some considerable time was to elapse before all the railways were completed. The GN was busy building other railways in the West Riding but this hardly accounts for the 10-year delay in opening the Headfield spur and the Dudley Hill-Low Moor line (the LYR positively shone by comparison, opening their admittedly small south curve at Low Moor during April 1886). Interestingly, a south curve was laid in by the GNR at Dudley Hill and completed by May 1894, but doubt exists if it was ever brought fully into use. One short length of LYR line which the GNR was not interested in using was the 3¾-mile Anchor Pit Junction-Pickle

Facing page, bottom:
A view of Cutlers Junction on 2 August 1963 with a Bradford-Goole DMU heading for Dudley Hill and Wakefield. The Pudsey line diverges to the right, and the connection to the Shipley line can be seen bearing right behind the signalbox.
M. York

Above left:
The worst of the climb is over, but 2-6-4T No 42196 still has to work hard past Armley Moor with the 10.20 King's Cross-Bradford on 29 April 1967. *M. Dunnett*

Below left:
A train to Bradford from the East Coast hurries away from Armley Moor behind Class '4MT' 2-6-0 No 43137 in August 1966. *L. A. Nixon*

Below:
A down freight approaches Beeston Junction on 13 March 1962 behind grimy 'B1' 4-6-0 No 61295.
G. W. Morrison

Above:
A view looking north from Batley station in the 1950s. From left to right the lines are the LNWR Birstall branch, the ex-LD&MR route to Leeds, the GNR line to Adwalton Junction and the remains of the GNR Tingley line. *K. Field*

Above right:
By August 1961 only one line remained at the derelict Woodkirk station.
M. Mitchell

Right:
Bradford's Manchester Road station in August 1970, seven years after closure to goods traffic and 55 years after the last passengers had left.
G. C. Lewthwaite

Facing page, top:
Great Horton in June 1961, with plenty of wagons around and the signalbox looking in remarkably good shape. *D. Butterfield*

Bridge connection, leaving the Calder Valley main line just west of Bradley and joining the Halifax-Bradford line at Wyke. The LYR ran a Bradford-Huddersfield service (using LNWR metals from Bradley Wood Junction), which involved a lengthy detour via Halifax, and this Pickle Bridge line was built as a cut-off route for traffic going to Huddersfield or beyond. The line could trace its origins back to the WRUR Act of 1846 which, of course, never saw the light of day. During the mid-1860s the LYR promoted a direct Halifax-Huddersfield line and revived the original scheme as a branch line only from Wyke, but arguments over land ownership delayed the Act until 1875. The direct line was dead by then, hence the branch was extended to Anchor Pit to form a through connection, and opening took place on 1 March 1881.

Shipley, Pudsey and Batley

The narrative of GNR events in the Calder and Spen Valleys from the late 1870s has brought us to the year 1893 rather too quickly, as many other events of great importance took place elsewhere in the Leeds and Bradford areas during this period. Whilst the LYR effectively retrenched itself to the wrong side of the Pennines, managerially speaking, the GNR marched onwards to dominate the West Riding suburban rail network. The end result of the GNR/LYR agreements of 1882-83 did not satisfy the railway users of the heavy woollen district as was originally hoped for — this point will be explained later — but elsewhere the GNR was busily building suburban lines regardless of engineering difficulties and also,

perhaps, regardless of any hope of future profitability.

An early example of one of these lines was the Laisterdyke-Shipley route, proposed in 1866-67 by two independent companies, the Bradford, Eccleshill & Idle Railway (BE&IR) and the Idle & Shipley Railway (I&SR). These outer villages on the eastern side of the city were built on high ground in open countryside, at a respectable distance from the smoke-wreathed mills which lay in the bowl of the city area some 300ft below. Prosperity took the wealthy textile men to live in these 'des res' suburbs of the later 19th century, and the GNR quickly connected them into their system. One journalist of the day expected that the new line 'will open out building sites for villas, with beautiful and extensive prospects over Aire-dale and the surrounding country for many miles'. Goods traffic was expected to be carried in sufficient quantity to ease congestion on the streets of Bradford, which were suffering due to the large amounts — several thousand tons annually — of limestone which were taken to the ironworks at Low Moor and Bowling. Some difficulty was found in raising the necessary cash, however — even when the GNR stepped in and supplied most of the capital for the BE&IR and I&SR schemes, the rest was not forthcoming from the independent companies — and eventually the GNR bought out the two companies and built the line itself.

Construction was started in August 1871 by T. J. Waller of Cardiff under the supervision of J. Fraser, the line's engineer. It was initially intended that the line would leave the Leeds line about 900yd out of Laisterdyke, but this would have involved reversal at the station for

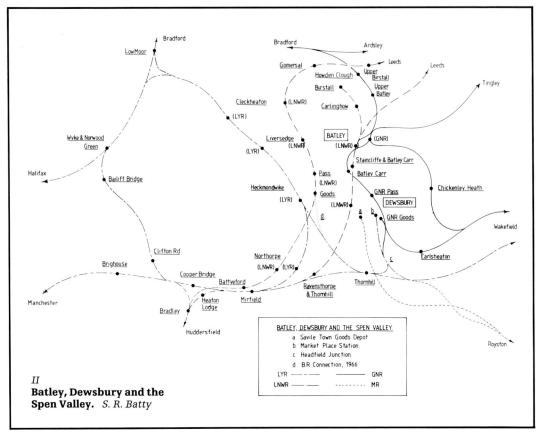

II
Batley, Dewsbury and the Spen Valley. *S. R. Batty*

Map labels: Bradford, LowMoor, Bradford, Ardsley, Gomersal, Leeds, Howden Clough, Upper Birstall, Leeds, Birstall, Upper Batley, Tingley, Cleckheaton, (LNWR), Carlinghow, (LYR), Wyke & Norwood Green, Liversedge, BATLEY, (GNR), (LNWR), (LYR), (LNWR), Halifax, Bailiff Bridge, Staincliffe & Batley Carr, Pass. (LNWR), Batley Carr, Heckmondwike, Goods, Chickenley Heath, (LYR), (LNWR), GNR Pass., DEWSBURY, d, a b, GNR Goods, Wakefield, Clifton Rd, Northorpe, (LNWR) (LYR), Earlsheaton, Brighouse, Cooper Bridge, Battyeford, c, Manchester, Heaton Lodge, Mirfield, Ravensthorpe & Thornhill, Thornhill, Bradley, Bradley, Huddersfield, Royston

BATLEY, DEWSBURY AND THE SPEN VALLEY
a Savile Town Goods Depot
b Market Place Station.
c Headfield Junction
d B.R. Connection, 1966
LYR —— · —   GNR
LNWR — ·· —   MR ········

any train going on to Wakefield and London. Direct access was provided by forking the line from Shipley at Quarry Gap Junction (after bridging the Leeds line), with one line going into Laisterdyke and the other meeting the Gildersome line at Cutlers Junction. The stations at Shipley & Windhill (so named at the request of the people of Windhill), Idle and Eccleshill were generally agreed to be of 'superior character' and of 'commodious, elegant appearance, far better than usual branch line stations'. Thackley station was built after the opening to passengers in April 1875, when eight trains daily (four on Sundays) made the 25min journey each way. The opening was greeted with general enthusiasm along the branch, and indeed the locals seem to have taken to the local pubs to celebrate the event — press reports speak of 'boozing' by men 'and a few ladies also'! Single fares from Bradford Exchange to Shipley were 8d first class and 6d second class.

Goods traffic flowed more heavily than the GNR had expected and included livestock and perishable goods as well as the expected coal, limestone and quarry stone. Plans to use the

Midland station at Shipley had fallen through and the GNR was compelled to build their own terminus next door. Initially the two were unconnected, but a short spur was laid in during 1875. Trains leaving Laisterdyke were not faced with a great deal of climbing towards Idle, but the descent to Shipley involved a long stretch at 1 in 61 which caused several locomotives to come to grief at Shipley over the years.

When the LBHJR was opened, in 1854, stations had been built at Armley & Wortley, Bramley, Stanningley and Laisterdyke, but the town of Pudsey was a good mile away from the railway at Stanningley. Pudsey is extremely hilly, and many complaints were made to the GNR about the difficulties involved in having to trudge on foot or transport goods by cart to Stanningley. By the 1870s Pudsey was doing very well in the trades of coal mining, stone quarrying and textile manufacture and, in July 1871, the GNR obtained an Act to build a branch line into the town. The 1¾-mile single-line branch curved away from the main line at Stanningley and was approachable only from the Bradford direction. Enough land was

Above:
'N1' 0-6-2T No 69434 gets away from Great Horton station with the 17.47 Bradford-Keighley on 14 May 1955. *J. F. Oxley*

Above left:
A Bradford-Keighley train passes the delightfully-named Paradise Green behind 'N1' 0-6-2T No 69478. *J. F. Oxley*

Left:
No 69434 arrives at Queensbury with a Keighley-Bradford train on 14 May 1955. *J. F. Oxley*

purchased to allow double-track to be laid if needed in future. Construction was not completed for almost seven years, and the sum of £101,289 5s 7d was expended before the public opening took place on 1 April 1878.

Even after all this time the advertised station at Pudsey Lowtown was still incomplete and passengers had to use the terminal station at Greenside, just a short distance away in Fartown. A total of 14 trains a day ran in each direction, the first leaving Stanningley at 06.10, and all the trains — particularly the evening ones — were crowded with passengers. Pudsey was not destined to remain as a dead-ended branch line, as the GNR/LYR agreement of 1883 resulted in more construction taking place. The GNR's Pudsey Act of 1871 allowed them to extend the line on from Greenside station to meet their Ardsley line at Tyersal — an idea which the LYR countered with a proposed Low Moor-Pudsey line at the same time, but which they allowed to lapse. This was taken up also, of course, after the agreement with the LYR. It would link up also, of course, with the Low Moor-Dudley Hill scheme, putting Pudsey on a new Leeds-Bradford loop and giving access to Halifax and the Spen Valley. At the other end of the branch a Leeds-facing connection was to be laid in at Bramley station. The GNR was apparently short of capital at this time, and the new lines were not completed until late 1893. Work at Pudsey involved enlarging Greenside station by building another platform, boring the 616yd Greenside tunnel, and forming a massive embankment (known as the Smalewell embankment) over Tyersal beck on the way to the north and south connections with the Gildersome line at Culters Junction and Broad

Lane Junction respectively (These two lines forked at Tyersal Junction.) The new line opened to passengers on 1 November 1893, one month before the GNR Dudley Hill-Low Moor section — delay was caused by a 70ft embankment slipping badly at Low Moor. Nine trains daily were diverted each way over the Pudsey loop, the first train from Bradford leaving Exchange at 07.50. If no loop train was available, passengers from Bradford could change at Bramley on to the next loop train from Leeds to Pudsey at no extra charge, whilst a similar arrangement allowed travellers to reach Bradford from Pudsey in the reverse direction. No similar arrangement appears to have been made for travellers from Leeds to change at Laisterdyke. At Bramley the new connection was brought into use and the original spur from Stanningley was disconnected at the Pudsey end, remaining in use as a siding.

As if the GNR did not have enough on their hands at this time, they also decided to take on the LNWR for a share of the traffic between the heavy woollen district and Leeds, principally from Dewsbury and Batley. They had a route (of sorts) from the two stations to Leeds via the Dewsbury loop, Ossett, Lofthouse and Ardsley, but this long-winded journey would be a non-starter in any competition with the LNWR's direct line to Leeds via Batley and Morley. So, they took the only possible course of action and applied for powers to build new lines to give them the route they wanted. Two short pieces of railway were planned, from Batley to Tingley on the Laisterdyke-Ardsley line, and from here down to Beeston on the Leeds-Wakefield line, and Acts were passed in July 1881 and July 1889 for the new lines.

Certainly an alternative Leeds-Dewsbury service could be operated over the proposed lines, but it is hard to see how the GNR ever hoped to compete with the LNWR. Whereas the latter's line had a stiff climb up to Morley tunnel, at least it was straight and relatively free of junctions compared with the GNR route which bore more resemblance to a mountain railway between Batley and Tingley than to anything the rival route had to cope with. Trains leaving Batley would have to climb at 1 in 50 through a 660yd tunnel at Soothill, turning and weaving on the way to Tingley. Here the Ardsley line

was briefly joined before swinging north and then descending to Beeston, crossing the Leeds-Wakefield line on a splendid viaduct before entering a flying junction which terminated at the new junction. The engineering work required was great indeed, particularly for a five-mile railway, and the financially pressed GNR must have had some hard times during the expansion years of the 1880s. Lack of money was probably the reason why the line took so long to build — opening to Soothill colliery took place in early 1888, but it was 1 August 1890 before the full passenger service

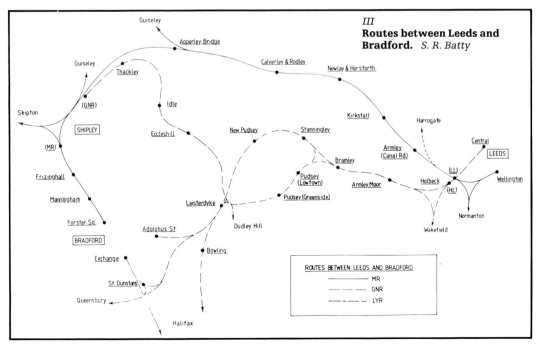

III
Routes between Leeds and Bradford. *S. R. Batty*

Class 150/2 Sprinter No 150246 climbs out of Bradford with the 10.40 Scarborough-Manchester on 27 January 1988. The infilled area to the right of the train is the site of the St Dunstan's complex, and the bridge in the foreground used to take the Queensbury line towards Manchester Road. *S. R. Batty*

Above:
Another Sprinter unit, No 150228, climbs past St Dunstans with the 13.00 Manchester-Scarborough on 27 January 1988. The bricked-up tunnel mouth was the route of the Queensbury line for trains running directly from Halifax to Leeds via this route. *S. R. Batty*

commenced. From November of that year a circular service was introduced from Leeds (Central) via Wrenthorpe Junction, Dewsbury, Batley and Tingley and some regular traffic between Leeds and Wakefield was diverted via Dewsbury and Tingley. Strongest competition with the LNWR was given over the Tingley-Leeds section where passengers from Morley could be whisked away via Beeston. Morley (GNR) station apparently left a great deal to be desired in the area of passenger comfort and not even reduced fares could tempt a majority of travellers away from the LNWR. The new GNR line was used as part of another circular service after the opening of the extended Pudsey line in late 1893, when seven trains daily in each direction left Leeds (Central) for a veritable rail-tour of the West Riding which took in Beeston, Tingley, Batley, Dewsbury, Thornhill, the L&YR Spen Valley stations, Low Moor, Dudley Hill, the Pudsey loop and thence back to Leeds! The Wrenthorpe circulars of 1890 origin lasted until 1938, but the 1893 extravaganza expired in 1914, perhaps not surprisingly.

The Queensbury Lines

For sheer difficulty of construction and operation the railways built by the GNR to Queensbury cannot be equalled in the West Riding. Very few remains are left today, but those features which have survived in this steep and rugged area leave the observer in no doubt of the tremendous problems which must have been faced by all concerned with building and running these lines. The land lies above the 1,000ft contour, the valleys are steep-sided and any excavation quickly exposes masses of rock. But several schemes for laying a railway

through this area to the west of Bradford had been tried long before the GNR finally completed their lines in 1884. The GNR involvement began 20 years earlier with a proposed Halifax-Keighley railway which was finally sanctioned as just 2½ miles of railway from Halifax to Holmfield, and in which the GNR and LYR had each invested one-third of the original capital. Difficulties started long before a single sod had been turned and dragged on to such a time- and money-absorbing extent that both companies took joint control of the railway from 1870, when construction started in earnest. Holmfield was reached in 1874.

Having got started on what would hopefully give them another route into Halifax, the GNR's next move was to open up a possible route from Bradford to Keighley which would also serve the textile manufacturers of Queensbury. Efforts were constantly being made to promote a railway from Huddersfield and Halifax to Keighley, and at several

attempts the MR had shown some interest but would not back any of the schemes with hard cash. The GNR naturally wanted to keep the MR out, and quickly took up the cause of the Bradford & Thornton Railway (B&T) in order to do this when the scheme went to Parliament in 1870. The B&T was backed by very strong local support from the Foster family of Queensbury, who originally wanted the line to go through to Keighley but had to settle for a Thornton line, at least for the time being, due to the same sort of engineering difficulties which had cut back the Halifax-Keighley plans of 1864. To safeguard their approach to Keighley (even though this may have seemed somewhat ambitious at the time) from any predatory attacks from the MR, the GNR took over the B&T in 1872. Meanwhile, the businessmen of Halifax battled on for a line to Keighley and after the MR finally backed out in October 1872 the promoters approached the GNR. They were told that Holmfield would be linked with Keighley if half the capital could

Gradient post at Hammerton Street Junction, 1987. *S. R. Batty*

be raised locally, and also that the GNR would not entertain building a railway into Huddersfield as requested by the Halifax party. This last point was unacceptable to the promoters, who promptly formed their own company, the Thornton & Keighley Railway (T&KR), to build on from the projected B&T line as well as northwards from Holmfield. The GNR must have once again seen the possibility of the MR gaining the prize, as they quickly offered to buy out the company and build on from Holmfield and Thornton. The offer was accepted, and the GNR was saddled with a capital requirement of some £650,000 for completion of the railways. What happened to the Huddersfield proposal is not clear, but presumably it was used as a bargain counter in the discussions with the GNR. The Bill was eventually passed by Parliament in May 1873 after some fierce competition from the Midland who, even though they had thrown away many opportunities to build these lines themselves, had objected to the schemes and even offered to build their own lines if the GNR Bill was thrown out!

Unfortunately events were slowed down by the severe economic depression of the 1870s. The B&T Act had been granted in July 1871 and at the amalgamation with the GNR during July 1872 it was stated that the line would hopefully be in use by August 1874. Reality dawned when work was eventually started during May 1874 at Queensbury tunnel, and also on the B&T proper, by the contractors Benton & Woodiwiss. Progress was painfully slow, and an extension of time was granted in 1876, but by November of that year the first section was opened from St Dunstan's, on the Leeds-Bradford line, to Great Horton station,

which included a goods branch to City Road. Clayton was reached by the summer of 1877, Thornton by April 1878. Construction from Holmfield to Queensbury, covering a distance of only 2¼ miles, was a nightmare. The 1 mile 741yd tunnel caused many problems due to water-bearing rock, but the 1,000yd long, 60ft deep Strines cutting which led into the tunnel from the Halifax end was much worse. Water flowed and gushed everywhere and landslips and pumping problems delayed the opening of the Halifax leg to Queensbury until 1 December 1879.

Passenger services from Bradford to Thornton started in October 1878, but by this time the GNR was suffering not only from the expense of building the lines from Halifax and Bradford, but also from the effects of the long trade depression of the 1870s. No work had started on the Thornton-Keighley section at this time, but the GNR decided to make a start on two of the most difficult items on the line, the tunnels at Lees Moor and Well Head. No further work was put in hand, and for some time the project was almost 'mothballed'. The great viaducts at Thornton, Hewenden and Cullingworth were all yet to be started, and the completion of the Keighley line was clearly some years into the future for any traveller who alighted on the Thornton platforms in 1879.

The GNR started a series of cost-cutting exercises in 1880, beginning with an approach to the MR to use a new joint station at Keighley rather than build a new GNR structure. This was approved in 1881, the GNR to approach the new station along a widened section of the Keighley & Worth Valley Railway (KWVR) from Ingrow. In return, the MR was granted some concessionary traffic from Keighley to Halifax. GNR goods traffic was to be handled in the company's own establishment, a rather splendid building just to the west of the KWVR line outside Keighley. Having reduced their financial burden somewhat, construction of the last leg started in 1881. Apart from the tunnels and viaducts which had to be built, trouble was experienced with landslips at Doe Park cutting near Denholme, where Bradford Corporation was concerned about the safety of one of their reservoirs! Opening took place to Denholme on 1 January 1884, and to Keighley by the following 1 November. Between Bradford and Keighley, stations were provided at Manchester Road, Horton, Clayton, Queensbury, Thornton, Denholme, Wilsden, Cullingworth and Ingrow (East).

Queensbury station was the most unusual on the line. Initially comprised of little more

Left:
The Bradford portion of the 'White Rose' descends to Exchange station past Hammerton Street behind 'B1' 4-6-0 No 61123. *K. Field*

Bottom:
Empty stock is propelled out of Exchange station by '4MT' 2-6-4T No 42650 on 3 September 1966. *D. Butterfield*

than bare, exposed platforms on all three sides of the triangle, and served by a steep and badly-lit access lane, the GNR spent some money in 1890 and greatly improved both the platforms and the public access. A signalbox was built at each corner of the triangle and the platforms were connected by a combination of footbridge, boarded crossing and subway. Main offices were placed on a footbridge at the Bradford end of the station, and two sidings for goods traffic were provided. From being an isolated textile village at 1,150ft above sea level, Queensbury had developed into a well-connected railway junction by the mid-1880s.

St Dunstan's station was opened in October 1875 on the Hammerton Street Junction-Mill Lane Junction section which gave access to Bradford Exchange station for the GNR traffic from Leeds. A forked connection was laid here which then passed under the LYR exit from Exchange and climbed steeply at up to 1 in 45 to Manchester Rd station. The City Road goods branch, a double-tracked stretch, left the line at Horton Park. Great Horton station was passed en route to Clayton, an island platform structure located just before one of the many short tunnels on this line. From Queensbury the Halifax line fell at 1 in 80 to Holmfield, and the Keighley line curved through an S-bend before traversing Thornton viaduct and then turning again into the island platform station. The section onwards to Keighley had the most spectacular engineering of all the lines, starting with Well Head tunnel just before Denholme. More short tunnels and a succes-

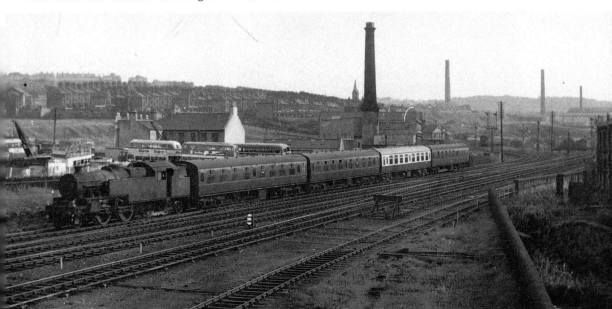

Right:
**'4MT' 2-6-4T No 42152 makes
a fine smoke display as she
leaves Exchange with the
Saturdays-only Poole train
on 26 August 1967.** *L. A. Nixon*

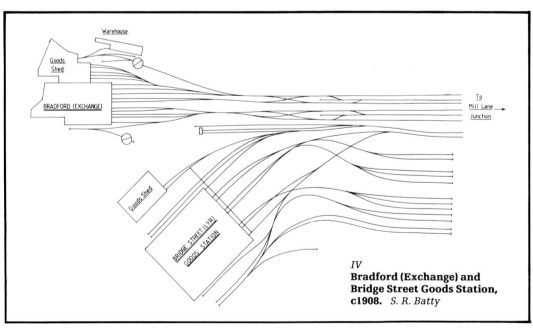

Warehouse

Goods
Shed

BRADFORD (EXCHANGE)

To
Mill Lane
Junction

Goods Shed

BRIDGE STREET (LYR)
GOODS STATION

IV
**Bradford (Exchange) and
Bridge Street Goods Station,
c1908.** *S. R. Batty*

sion of cuttings and embankments were made before Wilsden station was reached, the line now falling on an average gradient of 1 in 50 all the way from Denholme to Keighley. The viaducts at Hewenden (376yd long, 123ft high) and Cullingworth (150yd, 45ft) gave excellent views of the surrounding countryside before trains plunged into the 1,540yd gloom of Lees Moor tunnel, just beyond Cullingworth station. Trains entered the tunnel facing approximately westwards, but emerged having turned through almost a right angle to face Ingrow and Keighley. Just beyond Ingrow East station the line forked, passenger traffic then joining the KWVR line at Keighley GN Junction and then proceeding to the new joint station whilst goods traffic took the right fork which then burrowed under the KWVR line to reach the new goods depot.

A vast amount of money was absorbed in the building of the Queensbury lines and traffic levels were soon to be affected by the spread of Bradford's tram and bus network. Passenger takings were healthy until the turn of the century, but the new road competition quickly captured most of the short-distance traffic. The GNR's steep and hilly route to Keighley — known as the 'Alpine route' by train crews — could never seriously compete with the MR's easy gallop along the Aire Valley, and very few travellers would have chosen the GNR route from Leeds to Keighley, or from Leeds to Halifax via Queensbury.

Bradford Exchange Station

One further major GNR development took place in Bradford during the later years of the 19th century, that of building a branch line from Hammerton Street down to Mill Lane Junction to give access to the LYR station for joint use by the two companies (this development has already been mentioned briefly as a sequel to the 'Short line' story). The terminus at Adolphus Street was described as 'a lofty commodious structure, which though not overhandsome is well adapted for accommodating a large passenger traffic in every instance but one — it was built in the wrong place, where the traffic would not come, and hence the company have been compelled to go to the traffic'. This was written at the time of the GNR's transfer of passenger traffic to the recently-enlarged LYR station, known henceforth as Bradford (Exchange), in January 1867. To reach the station the GNR built the short branch line which included one tunnel and four bridges in its ¾-mile length. The branch left the LYR at Mill Lane Junction, curving

sharply eastwards, and passed over a tramway of the Bowling Iron Co before entering the short tunnel (132yd) under Hall Lane and Wakefield Road. At this point the Seven Stars public house had been demolished during construction work and nearby was the beginnings of Ripleyville, a model village being built by mill owners Ripley & Son for the benefit of their employees. The line was engineered by John Fraser and built by Samuel Pearson and construction work took no less than 18 months, due mainly to several old mine workings causing problems with the Wakefield Road tunnel. Pearson's main concern with the scheme was to exploit the vast amount of fireclay deposits uncovered during excavations — he set up a factory to produce bricks, tiles, chimney pots, drains etc from the 170,000cu yd of clay found, and provided work for 60 men over the following 15 years.

At the LYR station the main improvement which was made to accommodate the extra traffic was the building of a new island platform and the associated extension of the original one. Departures were to be made from the new platforms and arrivals would be directed to the old ones. The length of the lines was increased towards Leeds Road and new offices were built across the end of the building, which was also given a new raised roof to provide a little relief to the expected gloom and smokiness of the new terminus. Many felt that the station would be inadequate for the new levels of traffic to be handled. A total of about 125 trains in and out of the station was expected to be dealt with daily, made up of 30 LYR trains, 60 GNR trains, LYR goods traffic and market extras. The approach from Mill Lane was badly congested by the tunnel below Broomfield, and the need for a total station rebuild was seen by some as only a matter of time, with traffic levels quickly proving the case. An elevated signalbox was built at Mill Lane Junction, and the signals and points of the GNR and LYR companies were separated within the box and labelled accordingly. Col Yolland inspected the branch on Thursday 3 January 1867, and public services started on the following Monday. Trains took 30min between Leeds and Bradford, and the new S-shaped branch was generally agreed to have been built on an easy gradient of 1 in 59! The *Bradford Observer* was duly impressed by the effect of the new arrangements, and commented that 'The Lancashire & Yorkshire Station, during the week, has assumed an appearance of unusual liveliness'. Also noted was the near completion of the LYR hotel adjacent to the station which

Right:
A Class '5' 4-6-0 turns on St Dunstan's triangle.
M. Dunnett

was certain to be a boon to the town due to the shortage of good hotels in such a large and important manufacturing centre.

As many had expected, the altered station quickly showed itself to be inadequate for the new traffic levels. The alteration had been made at a reported cost of £8,000, which even with the benefit of 120 years hindsight does not sound a great deal of money to spend on such an important railway improvement. Perhaps the LYR — whose public image had reached rock-bottom by this time, and which was set to remain so for another 30 years — had simply been too frugal with the cash and ended up by getting no more than they had paid for. The station was dark, pungent and generally unpleasant, and a great deal of shunting was needed to assemble trains. In 1872 the LYR architect, Sturges Meek, drew up plans for a new station which would eliminate all the problems. The main features of the scheme were:

● Caledonia Street was to be bridged over the railway, and the present level crossing abolished.

● Broomfield tunnel to be opened out and the approaches greatly widened. This would involve building a large retaining wall on the eastern side of the new cutting and would also eliminate some of Bradford's worst slums.

● A new goods depot to be built on Bridge Street, allowing the existing one to be demolished to give more room for a much enlarged station.

Acts of Parliament were not granted until 1883 and 1884 and reasons for the long delay are not apparent. During this period a group of local people led by Eli Milnes, an architect, proposed the building of a brand-new Central station on a through line linking the MR and GN/LYR lines. They approached these companies, and also the NER and LNWR, for support, but the scheme was rejected as unworkable early in 1884. By August of that year the widening work was completed, the goods depot was almost finished and tenders were issued for building the new station. Work started early in 1885 and was completed by May 1888. Ten platforms covered by two 100ft arched roofs were provided and operated almost as two separate stations, with Platforms 1 to 5 devoted to LYR traffic and 6 to 10 being used by the GNR trains. A signalbox for each side was also built. The rebuilding had cost £300,000 and was generally thought to have been well worthwhile, but the new station was largely hidden from public view and, although horse-drawn traffic had a good entry and exit alongside the LYR platforms, passengers on foot still had to use a steep and gloomy staircase from Leeds Road.

4 Completion of the System

Improvements in Leeds

Within this period of time, which saw such great changes made in Bradford, there also took place some drastic alterations in the railway surroundings of Leeds. Whereas the changes in Bradford consisted largely of improving existing facilities, those in Leeds were concerned with new construction works which greatly altered the city's railway position. In the early 1860s those wishing to travel eastwards from the city, to Hull or York, were still saddled with the Hudson legacy which bound them to travel via Methley and Castleford and thence through Milford to either destination. The ex-L&S remained closed to passengers until 1850, when a Marsh Lane-Old Junction (ie Gascoigne Wood) service was reintroduced, but this served no purpose in giving a good Leeds-York/Hull service.

Congestion at Wellington station became severe, with traffic to and from all directions being concentrated in one narrow approach area. Marsh Lane station lay one mile eastwards across the city, a rather squalid dungeon of a place located amidst a very unappealing part of the town, but to the North Eastern Railway Co (NER) it pointed the way forward and was part of the solution to their Leeds problem. In 1864 the NER went to Parliament with a Bill to construct the required mile of railway to a new station on the north side of Wellington Street — in the same general area as had earlier been earmarked for one of the Central station buildings — cutting through a large swathe of commercial, industrial and domestic property. Such tremendous opposition to this was forthcoming that the company had to with-

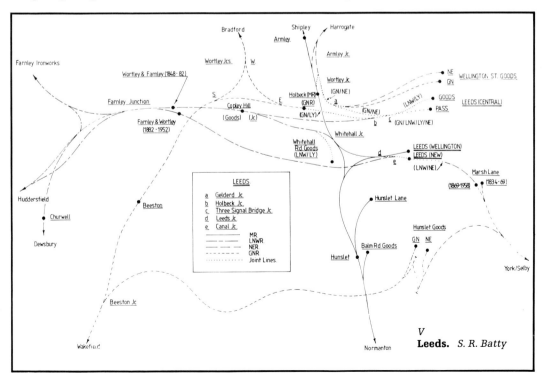

Leeds. *S. R. Batty*

Above:
A North Eastern 4-4-0 hurries eastwards through Crossgates around the turn of the century. The Wetherby lines diverge to the right.
Leeds City Libraries

draw the Bill, but they were (almost literally) on the right track. Other NER plans of the same period involved building on a very much grander scale, and two schemes are worthy of mention

1 To build a new line from Neville Hill through north Leeds and then down to a new Grand Central station in City Square, which would also be rail-connected to Central station.

2 Using the same Grand Central station but leaving Neville Hill and approaching via Hunslet, Holbeck and Holbeck Junction over Midland Railway metals before climbing at 1 in 88 to Central station, thence to Grand Central.

Both these plans were strongly opposed by Charles Leather, a veteran campaigner of the mania days who had grown to detest the NER, and were soon dropped, but the company allied itself with the LNWR before making a successful attempt with a Bill in 1865. The LNWR was being choked all along the line from Huddersfield to Leeds, and their involvement with Leeds (New) station was just one of several moves made by the company over the 35-year period to 1900 to improve the

Manchester-Leeds service. Leeds (Wellington) station, of 1853 vintage, was no longer capable of dealing with the volume and frequency of traffic being operated by the MR, the NER (to Harrogate) and the LNWR. Even the LYR ran into the station from Knottingley via Methley. A joint NER/LNWR Leeds (New) station would give the LNWR a little room to breathe once they had reached the station, and the simultaneously-proposed NER Micklefield-York cut-off line would give excellent access to the northeast. The NER was also intending to build the Cross Gates-Wetherby line, which would rid them of any dependence on the MR for access to the earlier route to Harrogate via Whitehall, Wortley and Armley Junctions.

The new station was certainly not an over-ambitious scheme, providing only one through platform and a bay at each end for the use of each of the operating companies, although the LNWR had two bay platforms with sidings in between by 1873. Travelling eastwards, the new railway to Marsh Lane traversed a considerable length of viaduct, much being alongside Leeds Parish Church and cemetery, and also cleared a way through some of the worst slums in Leeds. Double-track only was laid but it was expected that future congestion would demand another pair of tracks alongside, especially after the new Wetherby line was completed. Inspection was done by Col Hutchinson during late March 1869 and the LNWR and NER made a smooth removal of their offices to the new station on 31 March. Services commenced with no ceremony at all, the first departure being a mixed passenger and mail train which left for York at 02.16 amidst the explosions of a few fog signals placed on the line by a small band of well-wishers. During the day a large number of tickets were sold for the short journey to Marsh Lane, many people enjoying the novelty of a new cross-city journey, even though it was barely a mile in length. The changeover went very smoothly, not to say almost without being noticed at all, and the most remarkable feature commented upon at the time was the unusual sense of calmness which subsequently prevailed at Wellington station. The MR then began to contemplate improving their premises with better booking offices and an improved approach road — perhaps they were glad of the LNWR/NER departure to the new station too.

Architecturally the new station was a damp squib. Two roof spans covered the building, each covering platforms monopolised by each company. The station was carefully split into LNWR and NER operating areas, and it seems the two companies kept very much to themselves. Surprisingly, no through traffic was carried for many years until the advent of the Newcastle/Hull-Manchester/Liverpool through trains around the turn of the century. No interchange was made with the adjacent Wellington station either, which perhaps gave the impression that Leeds had just acquired two more main line stations which happened to be built on to the end of the existing MR terminus. The new building was almost completely hidden from public view and was generally thought to have made no contribution to the splendid appearance of the city centre which was then being created.

Traffic continued to flow into Leeds in ever greater quantities, and the two companies quickly realised that more development was needed at New station — so quickly was this appreciated that they had plans for a much larger station drawn up in time for the Parliamentary session of 1873/74, less than five years after the station was opened. How much of this need for yet more improvement was due to traffic levels, and how much was perhaps due to the inadequacy of the 1869 station, is not clear — one through platform and a couple of bays hardly qualifies as extravagance for a provincial city of such industrial and commercial output as was found in the Leeds of 1870. The parallel with the Bradford Exchange rebuilding is close, and it would seem that the same broad mistakes were made in both cases.

The extension of New station took several years to complete due to the large amount of

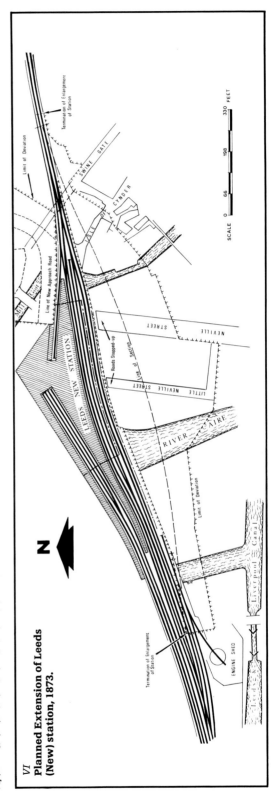

VI
Planned Extension of Leeds (New) station, 1873.

civil engineering made necessary by building out above the River Aire, the Leeds & Liverpool Canal, Neville Street, Little Neville Street and Swinegate. A great deal of property had to be bought up and demolished before the brick arches which were to carry the new works could be built. The original through road was cut into two more bay platforms and the area between was extended forward to a new through platform of equal length to the original, and this became the NER's principal platform at the new station. A subway was cut below the new lines to reach another new platform built on the southern side of the station, and independent goods lines were laid beyond this to take traffic which had previously rumbled through the main building. A third roof span was erected to cover the new work and a new approach road was built from Boar Lane, opposite Albion Street. Work was sufficiently complete to allow use of the extended area from Sunday 5 January 1879, by which date approximately £250,000 had been spent on the scheme by the LNWR and NER companies. Congestion at the station was greatly reduced (at last), and this arrangement was to survive almost 90 years before another

rebuilding took place for rather different reasons. Taking a momentary leap forward to 1989, it is true to say that today's Leeds station is, in terms of railway lines and sleepers, very little altered from the 1879 version. Obviously the layout has been simplified, but the basics remain unaltered.

Within the industrial West Riding, the LNWR might not have had anything like the total control of all services which they enjoyed in their own territory, but their Leeds-Huddersfield-Manchester line was a jewel which they constantly sought to improve by whatever means were reasonably possible. The Standedge route was shorter than the LYR line and the LNWR prided itself on the speed and quality of their trans-Pennine service. It was their only way into Leeds and it was their only way of making any profit from the city, and to their credit they did not abuse their monopolistic position. Spending about £250,000 as their share of the Leeds improvements between 1869 and 1879 still did not, however, give them the freedom from congestion which they wanted along the Manchester-Leeds run. In 1878 they promoted a completely new main line between the cities, but this failed primarily because of the large amount of housing which would have had to have been demolished along the way. One of the LNWR's greatest complaints centred on Whitehall Junction, where trains from Manchester would be held awaiting a path into Leeds New over MR metals. The LNWR paid the MR an

Below:
A Liverpool-Scarborough express speeds through Marsh Lane cutting behind a Class 47/4 locomotive early in 1988. *S. R. Batty*

annual rental of £6,500 for use of this short piece of line and felt they were getting a distinctly bad deal. Trains were regularly delayed — the LNWR alleged they were frequently signalled against as a matter of course — connections to the NER were missed, and the bad service was operating against the public interest. Their solution was to apply for powers to build a new line from Farnley into Leeds (New), largely on a viaduct and for use exclusively by passenger traffic. An Act was granted and the foundation stone was laid by Mrs H. C. Findlay, wife of the resident engineer to the works, on 16 December 1879. The viaduct was ¾-mile long, consisting of 83 brick arches, and 10 iron girder bridges of 80-90ft span were also built. Inspection was carried out by Maj Marindin, who insisted that each girder bridge was tested by having six locomotives parked thereon, and opening took effect from 1 March 1882. Wortley & Farnley station was moved from its 1848 site on the original line into Leeds (Central) and reopened as Farnley & Wortley on the end of the new railway. The junction to the west of Leeds New was called Canal Junction, and regular passenger traffic over the Farnley-Copley Hill-Whitehall Junction line ceased, freight traffic, of course, remaining. So was created the 'Viaduct Route', for an expenditure of approximately £100,000, and the LNWR had at last gained an independent access to the station at the end of their Leeds branch.

Developments continued, however, which made sure that the building of the Leeds viaduct was to become only the start of a long story. Freight traffic was clogging the Heaton Lodge-Thornhill section, and the gradients to Standedge ensured slow progress for a large amount of freight traffic which inevitably caused delays to the express workings between Leeds and Manchester. Widening was the only answer which would allow the LNWR to run prestige passenger trains and also keep a large share of the freight business. The opening of Leeds viaduct was followed by widening work at Huddersfield (where a new station was opened in 1886), quadrupling between Thornhill and Heaton Lodge by the LYR, also by the LNWR to Marsden by 1891, and by new tunnels at Huddersfield (1886) and Standedge (1894). Even the section from Diggle down to Stalybridge was increased to four-track capacity by the construction of the Micklehurst loop, opened to passenger traffic in 1886. All this improvement work was thwarted in its full effectiveness by the limitations of the Thornhill-Leeds section, where civil engineering difficulties — par-

Below:
The Wetherby line gave access to Harrogate for the NER without any use of running powers. 'Hunt' class 4-4-0 No 62738 *The Zetland* **approaches Leeds at Whitehall Junction, using the ex-L&BR tracks, with a local train from Harrogate in the 1950s.** *K. Field*

Congestion at Whitehall badly affected LNWR services into Leeds. Class '5' 4-6-0 No 44901 takes the 10.20 Sheffield (Midland)-Bradford (Forster Square) past the ex-LNWR lines on 13 April 1963.
G. T. Robinson

ticularly the Morley tunnel — and lack of available land ruled out any widening scheme. So the LNWR again applied for powers to build a new line, but this time the railway would run from Heaton Lodge to Farnley, just outside Leeds, and would also serve the Spen Valley towns en route (perhaps the failure of the GNR/LYR agreement of 1882 to give a decent Leeds/Huddersfield field service to the valley had helped the LNWR to make the decision). The chosen route was certainly a difficult one, with steep gradients and tight curves at all points except the extremities, where a gentle approach at Heaton Lodge and a split flying junction at Farnley connected the New Line (as it was to be known) to the existing LD&MR line. The Bill was presented to Parliament in 1892 and the Act was granted on 27 June, despite opposition from the LYR who wanted the LNWR to use their line from Mirfield up the valley to Cleckheaton, and then build on to Leeds. The LNWR lost no time, and construction went ahead promptly, but it was 1900 by the time the line was finally opened. Many cuttings had to be blasted out of solid rock, several large bridges and viaducts were

required and the tunnel at Gildersome was almost as long and difficult to bore as its near neighbour at Morley. Stations were built at Gildersome, Upper Birstall, Gomersal, Cleckheaton, Liversedge, Heckmondwike, Northorpe and Battyeford. Goods depots were initially built ready for the opening to goods traffic on 9 July 1900 at Gildersome, Upper Birstall, Gomersal and Northorpe, and only Battyeford was not given any goods facilities at all when the other stations were so equipped by November of the same year. Passenger traffic started from 1 October, when stopping trains were introduced. A total of 12 stopping trains ran each way, taking about 1hr for the Leeds-Huddersfield journey, and it is interesting to note that at its opening, the New Line was specifically intended to benefit Spen Valley passengers who wished to reach Leeds or Huddersfield. It was not built as an express route from Leeds to Manchester, and no through trains were provided. Local traffic was the target (which could either feed into the LNWR proper at Huddersfield, or simply enjoy the service to Leeds which they had wanted for so many years), along with a healthy goods haulage trade as witnessed by the generous provision of goods sheds. By diverting away much of the freight and slow passenger traffic over this hilly route, the easier Dewsbury route would be better able to handle the fast express traffic.

At the other end of New station the NER

found that some improvements were needed to handle the increased traffic flows, much as had been expected in 1869. The two-track section out to Marsh Lane could not be widened but the Richmond Hill tunnel could certainly be improved by the relatively simple method of removing it and laying extra tracks. This work was duly undertaken, and was completed during 1895 when today's Marsh Lane cutting was brought into use.

Leeds New station itself featured in one of the most destructive fires known in the city during 1892. The rebuilding of 1879 involved the construction of a great many arches and vaults above the river and canal, and many of these were used as industrial premises and warehouses. The Dark Arches were well known for the stinking foul water which flowed through them and for the villainous characters who inhabited the area, and the true cause of the

Above:
Leeds (New) station in April 1962. *J. S. Whiteley*

Left:
Class 'G5' 0-4-4T No 67262 ends her days as pilot at Leeds (New) in August 1958. *M. Mitchell*

fire was never established. Six arches were used by Joseph Watson & Co for the making of soap, and large quantities of soap and palm oil were held in their factory. The arches had apertures in the roofs, and it was suggested afterwards that some hot ash had fallen down from the railway into the soapworks and started the fire. This was discovered at 04.00 on 13 January by Thomas Coward, a night watchman at a nearby slate merchant's premises, and although the fire brigade were on the scene within 20min, the resulting fire burned for two days and caused a great deal of destruction. First to succumb was a MR wooden carriage shed, followed by the partial collapse of some platforms and twisting of the 80yd wide girder bridge across the canal. Casualties were fortunately very few, but one fireman from the MR was killed in the platform collapse. The services of the LNWR and NER were hit badly, but the MR lines at Wellington were unaffected. The GNR offered facilities at Central station, but the NER managed by using Holbeck station and also the unaffected eastern end of New station. Traffic was sent to the northeast via Wetherby instead of the more usual Horsforth route. Presumably the LNWR

made use of their still-valid running powers into Central station.

Changes at Bradford

On the original railway of the L&BR the later years of the 19th century were not without incident or improvement. Perhaps the most notable incident was the collapse of Apperley viaduct, across the River Aire, in November 1866. Heavy rainfall during that month had turned the Apperley Bridge-Esholt part of the valley into a gigantic lake with a relentlessly-moving stream at the centre. By Friday 16 November only the taller trees and the 10 arches of the viaduct were just clear of the tide, and during that afternoon the flood became stronger than ever. One pier was built on an island in the river, with the riverbed below the adjacent arches, and the water was scouring away the soft, light foundation material during that afternoon. At 17.00 the guard of a Bradford-Leeds train told the stationmaster at Apperley Bridge that the viaduct was unsafe, and all signals were immediately put to danger. Unfortunately a luggage train was approaching rapidly and could not be stopped in time — despite the

stationmaster running across the viaduct to attract the driver's attention — and this train drew to a halt on the third arch. This light train of only two vans and a guard's van caused the arch to quickly sink by 18in, upon which the crew quickly ran for safety. After 15min the arch collapsed and the wooden vans were swept away, leaving only the sunken locomotive and tender. By the prompt action of the local train guard a catastrophe had been avoided, and no injury or loss of life was involved.

What followed was almost a rebuilding miracle. The next day's weather was much improved and the MR built a 5yd wide footbridge across the gap, complete with full lighting, and processions of passengers detrained to use the footbridge to reach a connecting service on the far side. Rebuilding was done by 400 men contracted by Benton & Woodiwiss, who completed the job in just seven weeks. A new bridge of 60 girders and 150 plates was built by Butler & Pitts of Stanningley using material supplied by the Monk Bridge Iron Co of Leeds. Normal services were resumed from 3 January 1867, and the *Bradford Observer* recorded their appreciation

of the speedy repairs in the following terms:

'The Midland Railway Company, and all parties concerned, are to be congratulated upon the promptitude and energy which have characterised their proceedings since the destruction of the viaduct by the late flood.'

This part of the Aire Valley suffered from yet more violent weather in 1872. On 16 June a thunderstorm of great violence rapidly flooded Thackley tunnel to a depth of 2ft, and an up express was blocked in when lightning brought down much of the stonework at the Apperley Bridge end and blocked the track. Once again, the MR responded quickly and decisively, and 100 men were promptly despatched from Leeds to clear up the mess. Normal service was resumed by midnight. At the time of these incidents only double-track was laid from Leeds to Shipley, but traffic grew so rapidly — especially after 1876 when the new Settle & Carlisle line was opened — that this stretch was quadrupled by 1900 and a second bore at Thackley was opened, together with further crossings of the river and canal en route.

Until 1876 Leeds and Bradford were nothing

more than cities at the extremity of the MR empire — apart from the Lancaster line, there was not really anywhere else to go beyond the two cities. The Settle & Carlisle changed this state of affairs drastically, with Anglo-Scottish expresses suddenly running through Leeds and Shipley, and also bypassing Bradford. Two features of Bradford's railway history are directly related to this new route to Glasgow and southwest Scotland, the first being the long overdue renewal of Market Street station. The new six-platform Bradford station came into use at 12.00 on Tuesday 4 March 1890 without any ceremony. Two spans of an iron and glass roof were placed between the station walls with a row of columns along the centre, and a 'Renaissance' appearance was continued in features of stone and lightly-coloured brickwork. The total platform length was ¾-mile, some allowing three trains to use one platform simultaneously. Heavy traffic such as was experienced on market days and bank holidays was

expected to see 15 trains being handled at one time. Much growth and improvement had taken place in the city centre, and Trubshawe's elegant frontage was generally agreed to be in good harmony with the new post office, shops, warehouses and greenery which had been placed in Forster Square. The new hotel adjacent to the terminus was due to be completed soon, and one local journalist thought that the result would be the best traffic centre in the country, if not in Europe! Bradford, he thought, had risen in railway terms from a fifth-rate town on a tenth-rate branch line to one of the country's best. He wrote that the scale of structure, equipment and electric lighting had 'made a wonderful transformation scene upon the melancholy shed which during a generation has given hundreds of thousands of people their first dismal idea of Bradford'.

Exchange station was still very new at this time, and he observed that travellers to either station would no longer want to take the first train back in order to escape such gloom and misery as had been offered by the original structures. The new Midland station was provided with several docks for loading and unloading of horses and carriages behind the hotel, and a fish dock was built with its own approach road. The aforementioned 'melancholy shed' became part of a new goods depot. Even though Bradford was at the end of a

Below:
Class 40 No D271 hauls the 15.16 Newcastle-Liverpool away from Gildersome Tunnel and up the 1 in 90 to the New Line summit at Birstall on 3 August 1964. This line featured some tremendous earthworks within its 13-mile length. *M. Mitchell*

2¾-mile branch from the main line at Shipley, it now had a station of sufficient capacity, elegance and dignity to grace any main line establishment. The MR had not been slow to appreciate the potential of the city and the need for rebuilding — the necessary land had been purchased as long ago as 1874, but work had not started until 1884 — and their plans for Bradford certainly did not end in the year 1890.

The Cross-Bradford Scheme

The desirability of building a connecting railway across Bradford city centre to join the lines between Shipley and Low Moor has been apparent ever since the two systems first faced each other across a gap of approximately 300yd. It might as well have been 300 miles. After the failure of the WRUR cross-town scheme in 1846, the next serious attempt was put forward by the LYR in 1865. Their idea was to build a new joint GNR/LYR/MR station, and was probably prompted by the increasingly apparent shortcomings of their own Bradford terminus. Eventually all partners withdrew and, as the LYR alone could not stump up the estimated cost of £260,000, the idea failed. In 1874 the MR proposed a Huddersfield-Bradford line which would have run via Low Moor to Frizinghall, at a cost of approximately £1.5 million. The company bought the necessary land at Frizinghall and presented a Bill to

Left:
A New Line milepost in 1988, 23 years after closure. MP13 nestles in the undergrowth at Farnley. *S. R. Batty*

Parliament on 21 May 1874. It was rejected 13 days later, but the seed of a great MR idea had been sown.

The idea of a new, central joint station was raised again in 1883 when the MR invited the Bradford Town Clerk to Derby to consider proposals for another cross-city railway. This was sponsored by the Council and Chamber of Trade, but again the idea floundered. Then, in 1894, a deputation from Huddersfield, Halifax and many smaller West Riding towns went to Derby to exert pressure on the MR to build new lines which would give them much better north-south links than those provided by the GNR and existing MR routes. After a great deal of deliberation the MR concluded that rich pickings were to be had by building a new railway from their main line at Royston to Thornhill, where diverging new lines would reach one way to Halifax and Huddersfield, and also via the Spen Valley to Bradford. By 1896 the route was surveyed (saving 11½ miles between St Pancras and Bradford) and the Act for the MR (West Riding Lines) was passed on 25 July 1898. The MR hoped to gain much better penetration of the West Riding at the same time as they were improving their Anglo-Scottish main line, but many questions were raised by the scheme. Stations were planned for Thornhill, Heckmondwike, Liversedge, Cleckheaton and Oakenshaw — would the LYR quietly accept such competition? As the LNWR was then building its Leeds New Line, how could these towns possibly support no less than three stations each? What upheaval would be needed in the area around Bradford's showpiece of Forster Square? And would the Halifax/Huddersfield line eventually be pushed northwards, as the inhabitants desired, to reach Keighley or Hellifield?

The railway was to be built initially in two sections, Royston-Thornhill (8¼ miles) and Thornhill-Bradford (11 miles) for a total cost of £2.1 million. Many roads would have to be stopped up, bridges and viaducts of all sizes and shapes would be required, and some fearsome tunnelling would be needed before the former L&BR route was reached at Frizinghall, as in the 1874 scheme. Work started at Royston in 1902 and the straightforward section to Thornhill was finished by

Above:
The Leeds end of Gildersome tunnel, 1988.
S. R. Batty

Below:
'Type 2' (later Class 25) diesel No 5235 passes Manningham with a St Pancras-Bradford (Forster Square) train on 23 October 1966.
C. T. Gifford

Bottom right:
The 15.40 Carlisle stopper gets under way from Forster Square behind 'Britannia' No 70001 (formerly *Lord Hurcomb*) in April 1966.
J. S. Whiteley

10 November 1905. By 3 March 1906 a goods line was built into Dewsbury Savile Town Yard and a spur was connected on to the LYR main line at Thornhill, and at this point the MR board called a halt to the works on the Bradford line. In 1907 the MR obtained running powers over the LYR towards Huddersfield, but the LNWR blocked any progress beyond Heaton Lodge and the MR then built their own branch from Mirfield to Huddersfield (Goods), opened in November 1910. The Bradford line would have involved a Calder Valley viaduct at Dewsbury, a tunnel under Dewsbury Moor and a great tunnel of at least 5,000yd from Low Moor below Bierley Top, Bowling Park, Ripleyville and Broomfields and then under a covered way below Forster Square, through underground platforms below Midland station and finally emerging 150yd beyond at Manningham Junction.

Why did the MR suddenly abandon its new main line? Briefly, it would seem that the engineering problems involved in driving the railway from Low Moor to Frizinghall, coupled with the economic climate of the times, gave the MR a sharp attack of cold feet. In February 1905 the Midland told their shareholders that no further progress was possible with the line, beyond that which was (then) almost completed to Thornhill. In the following April a deputation from Bradford was told of serious engineering difficulties foreseen along the route, and of the low rate of return which the new line was expected to yield. The 1898 Act had secured the water rights for Ripley's mill, which bound the MR to maintain the supply at all times regardless of any tunnelling work or excavation on their line. This may seem to be a

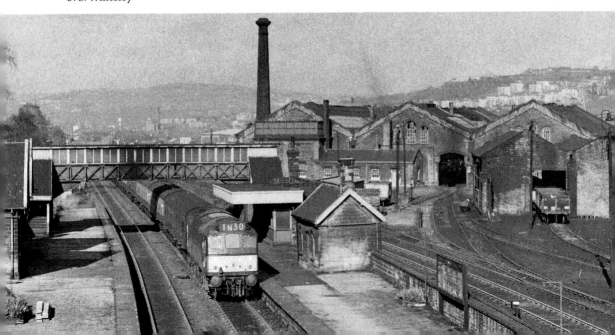

trivial point upon which to hang the fate of such a venture, but it would seem that the difficulties and cost of maintaining this supply of water proved too great to overcome. Water had been the great problem for endless tunnels over the years, and the usual solution was to lead the drainage away to the nearest watercourse. Here, though, the problem was somewhat different — no doubt the underground streams could have been led out of the tunnel, but in doing so many mills (including Ripley's) would have lost their supplies. A mill without water is a mill without steam power, hence the clause in the Act to protect Ripley's supply.

On the economic front, times had changed since 1898. The MR's Act was granted at a boom time for railways, but the aftermath of the Boer War led to a recession which made the MR think very hard before spending millions of pounds on the new line. The line to Thornhill was built to standards which would allow the heaviest flows of traffic to be carried, and this would not be justified by ending up in goods yards at Dewsbury and Huddersfield — the MR clearly did intend reaching Bradford when work started. Another incentive to continue lay in the swathes of land which the MR had bought in the city to make way for the line. By 1906 much of this had lain derelict for nearly 10 years, and the resale value was negligible. Rateable values had plummeted too, adding to the gloom at the Town Hall and Chamber of Trade. Leeds had recently been racing ahead in terms of city development, due largely to its excellent railway connections, and Bradford now appeared once again doomed to remain at the end of a siding,

perhaps forever. Should they now press the MR to proceed with the scheme, and extend the time available for completion, or should the idea be simply abandoned? The only course was to gain Parliamentary approval for an extension of time and to allow the MR to modify the scheme in order to avoid the problems of the original plan. One suggestion was that the Corporation should take a large financial stake in the venture and so assume control, but the idea was not taken up (this was prompted by recent similar moves in Manchester, where Corporation money had been pumped into the ailing Ship Canal Co which then became a moneyspinner).

A revised plan was then drawn up by the MR which eliminated the worst of the tunnelling and instead used viaducts and an elevated railway with high-level platforms at Midland station. Trains would run via the LYR Spen Valley line to Oakenshaw, south of Low Moor, where the new line would diverge towards the city. One mile beyond here lay the entrance to a 3,600yd tunnel to Ripleyville, passing below Bierley and Bowling Park. A second short tunnel then followed, below Broomfields and Wakefield Road, followed by a cutting to the north of Diamond Street which led on to a viaduct. This structure would have radically altered the centre of Bradford had it ever been built. Many roads and streets would have been stopped up and much property would have been demolished. The arches would have allowed a headroom of only 15ft, except over Leeds Road, where 25ft was to be allowed to clear the tram route, and over Forster Square, where a similar clearance would bring trains to high-level platforms above Platforms 5 and

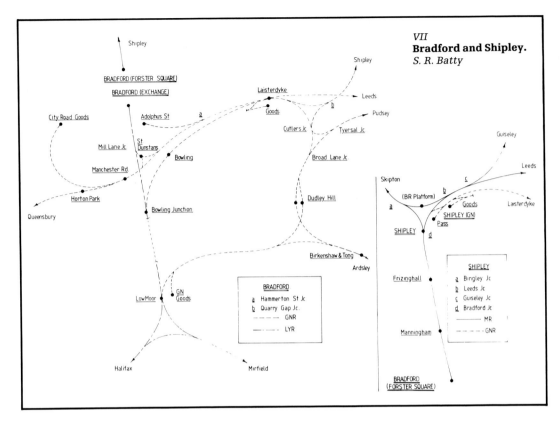

6 in Midland station. The line would then be slewed slightly to avoid the Trafalgar Brewery before reaching Manningham Junction. The estimated cost of the revised scheme was £815,667, but even this reduced budget failed to prod the MR into any action with pick and shovel. By October 1910 the construction period had been extended on four occasions, and the only progress which had been made towards a direct St Pancras-Bradford service was the provision of three expresses daily each way running via the LYR Spen Valley route and the new Royston line, with the LYR hauling the trains to and from Sheffield. Some doubts clouded the picture when the full implications of the altered scheme were appreciated — the overhead railway would not only be an aesthetic disaster for the city, but it would also involve a considerable loss of income from rates on demolished property. Dewsbury's town leaders were unimpressed at being left out, and the Spen Valley route was already close to choking point with traffic, and some opposition to the scheme was heard from these areas. Nevertheless, Bradford wanted a new railway and eventually resorted to some very expensive carrot-dangling to implore the MR to finish the line, overhead railway included.

The Corporation offered an annual rate reduction on the new works of £8,000 for 20 years, a price which many thought was too high when weighed against the as-yet unconfirmed benefits to be gained. It was a hard bargain, but the Midland then went to Parliament and received their new Act on 25 July 1911, despite opposition from the Spen Valley/Dewsbury area.

Many voices were then raised expressing concern over the plan. As well as agreeing to demolish property, stop up roads and build a viaduct through the town, the Corporation was going to subsidise the Midland's railway at a very hefty expense to the ratepayers. But above all else, one very simple, unanswered question remained — how much traffic would be sent over the new line? Leeds was a long established and highly important part of the MR empire which had been on their Anglo-Scottish route for over 30 years by this time. How much traffic would be diverted away from here to run over a choked LYR secondary line before crossing Bradford on a railway which would never be expanded or ever offer the smallest goods shed for use en route? Through passenger traffic would certainly benefit, but the majority of express trains would always

use the Leeds route, where quadruple track was available from Sheffield to Skipton.

Time moved on, still without any material developments. Local concern led a Bradford architect, John Ledingham, to draw up plans for making the best use of the overhead railway viaduct. He proposed a stone-built structure amidst new buildings and roads which would blend as well as possible with the existing surroundings and maintain many through roads — no-one wanted a steel girder and blue brick monstrosity which would appear as if it had been built, roughshod, on top of the existing city centre. The MR bought the Trafalgar Brewery in order to avoid a kink in the line on the way to Manningham, but all these developments came to naught with the outbreak of war in August 1914. After being shelved during the war years the scheme was revived briefly during 1918, but the good years

Above:
The MR's blue brick viaduct at Crigglestone remains intact in 1988. *S. R. Batty*

Left:
Class '4MT' No 43070 plods through Frizinghall on the down slow line with a freight on 13 May 1959. *D. Butterfield*

Above:
**The 'G5' 0-4-4T locos were used for suburban
work in their earlier years, but No 67262 is seen
here leaving Leeds (City) for Harrogate in early
BR days, towards the end of her working life.**
E. Treacy

had gone and the MR dropped the plan once
and for all. Postwar inflation and poor returns,
together with the pre-1914 doubts, and the
widened Leeds route, put an end to the
Bradford Through Line. The scheme was
formally abandoned on 18 November 1919, and
for the second time in 70 years the city had lost
the chance of having a through main line built
across the town centre. There was certainly no
lack of effort on the part of the city authorities
in trying to get the railway built, but outside
influences conspired against them and caused
the failure of the plan. If the early years of the
century had been more prosperous, and if the
events of 1914 had not occurred, then Bradford
would have had its new line and the
railways of the West Riding would have been
radically altered right up to the present day.

Some Train Services, 1900-1914

Eight miles away to the east (as the crow flies)
railway development in Leeds during the

period 1900-1914 saw the city rise to a position
of importance equalled only by a very few
other much larger centres throughout the
United Kingdom. The city was the railway
crossroads of the country (served by the GNR,
NER, MR, LNWR and GCR) and the frequency
of services and connections provided at Leeds
were unrivalled across the country. Wellington
station was little improved from its original
1844 state and the shabby appearance drew
many comments about the position of such a
dilapidated shed amidst the fine new buildings
which had recently been erected around City
Square. Shabby or not, the MR certainly
handled plenty of traffic — a total of 120
arrivals and 116 departures took place every
24hr during 1903, with the longest pause in
activity taking place between the arrival of an
up 'Scotchman' at 23.30 and a West of England
departure at 00.10. The 'Scotches' were the
MR's crack expresses through Leeds, giving a
fastest time to St Pancras of 3hr 47min. Some
of these expresses did bypass Leeds station for
a short time, travelling from Holbeck direct to
Whitehall Junction, and providing a connection at Armley, but this service was not
popular and did not survive. Reversal at
Wellington was avoided, however. Competition with the GNR for London traffic was
always intense, but the natures of the two

main lines always gave the advantage of speed to the GNR service from Central station. The MR route was congested, and such towns as Sheffield, Nottingham and Leicester could not be completely ignored. Opening of the Manton/Nottingham line gave some improvement, but the GNR's shorter mileage and uncongested, faster route still could not be beaten. Not everyone wanted to get to London as quickly as possible, and many travellers preferred the MR's 'jog-trot' pace to the awe-inspiring high-speed gallop of the GNR. The GNR's fastest train was the 14.00 to King's Cross which took 3hr 35min and which also apparently converted one or two less-seasoned travellers to the merits of the MR's slower but gentler rate of travel! Going northwards, the principal expresses to Carlisle departed at 10.00 and 13.28, with return workings made later in the day. Two Midland Compound 4-4-0 locomotives, Nos 2631 and 2632, and believed to be amongst the heaviest in the country at the time, were based at Leeds for these duties.

Holiday traffic was not particularly lucrative for the MR. Their services from Leeds and Bradford to Morecambe faced competition from the LNWR and LYR, and many people from either city travelled via other companies to other resorts — from Bradford to Blackpool or Southport via the LYR, or from Leeds to Scarborough or Bridlington via the NER. The Leeds-Sheffield run was a MR monopoly, but it certainly was not renowned for speed. Most trains took about 50min for the journey, hampered by an endless succession of junctions and subsidence restrictions along a route which was crowded with traffic. The Manchester, Sheffield & Lincolnshire Railway (MSLR) had operated a competing service in the 1880s running via Wakefield, Hemsworth (along the WRG line) and Rotherham (via the Swinton & Knottingley Joint line), but this fizzled out rather quickly. It must have been a fast and furious journey with all efforts put into sheer speed and very little, if any, put into considerations of passenger comfort. Contemporary accounts refer to the service as being 'the best thing for the liver ever prescribed' and also as being 'infinitely superior to horse exercise'. Sam Fay revived the service in 1902, providing three trains daily each way which

took 63-70min for the trip. Clearly these were not intended as competition for the MR. The Great Central Railway (GCR) was busily expanding in the south and west, and these trains formed connections into Fay's cross-country network reaching to the south coast, South Wales and the southwest.

Wellington station's dinginess did, however, conceal one gem in the form of the Dressing Room. This was one of the first such establishments opened about 1902 and placed in the care of a Mr Faulkner. A traveller could have buttons sewn or even buy a complete stock of linen. Mr Faulkner's boast was that 'He can be hatted, booted, gloved, spurred, showered, shampooed, and have his hair cut as well as be manicured and pedicured'. Wonderful!

The Aire Valley route was widened between 1901 and 1906 to try and keep the local trains, the goods traffic and the Scotch expresses flowing as freely as possible. Guiseley Junction to Apperley Junction was quadrupled (including the second bore at Thackley tunnel) by October 1907, and the work was extended to Newlay by August 1904 and to Kirkstall by March 1906. A third pair of tracks was built as a flyover from Kirkstall to Armley Canal Junction by 1909, such was the congestion along the Whitehall Junction-Shipley section (the southernmost pair of tracks was designated as the fast lines). Passengers between Bradford and all other points on the MR main line still faced awkward connections to or from Market Street — most passengers changed trains either at Leeds or Hellifield. In 1907 the MR introduced a trial service centred on Apperley Bridge station, which involved running a local train from Bradford to provide connections into up and down expresses which

were stopped at the station. Bradford passengers from the north and south would change on to the local (which also detrained passengers from Bradford into the main line trains), which then returned some 20min after arrival. The idea did not prosper and was soon discontinued. The trial was done with only the one local train, running in the mid-afternoon — one wonders why a more comprehensive service was not provided throughout the day.

Passenger services between Leeds and Bradford were an area of head-on competition between the MR and the GNR. The ex-L&BR route was very much the 'country' line, with the fastest locals taking 20min for the $13\frac{1}{2}$-mile trip along the levels of the Aire Valley. By 1914 the MR's Bradford station — still viewed as an elegant piece of architecture, albeit at the end of a branch line — was dealing with 36 daily arrivals from Leeds and despatching 33 back, with a couple of Saturday extras. Most trains took 25min, with the slowest taking 40min, and were powered by 0-4-4 tank locomotives or 2-4-0 or 4-4-0 tender machines. Apart from the three 20min expresses, all trains stopped at Shipley. Matters were rather faster and more furious on the competing GNR line, where tramway competition was making itself felt all the way from Leeds to Bradford via Armley, Bramley, Stanningley, Pudsey and Laisterdyke. To counter this threat all trains not taking the Pudsey loop stopped at Stanningley, and all trains for Leeds stopped at Holbeck High Level regardless of their route from Exchange station. The 'Short Line' was a difficult route for engine crews, with the viciously steep climb out of Bradford to Laisterdyke being complemented by a long, hard pull out of Leeds which climbed at 1 in 50 to Armley and

Left:
Another 'D49/2', No 62774 *The Staintondale* of Starbeck shed, takes water at Leeds City on 7 August 1956.
G. W. Morrison

1 in 100 from Bramley. In 1902 the GNR introduced an intensive service which included express trains covering the 10½ miles in 17min, inclusive of the Stanningley and Holbeck stops. A total of 30 trains ran each way daily and the stopping trains took 28min via Stanningley or 32min via the Pudsey loop. Some trains operated only between Leeds and Pudsey and between Bradford and Bramley. Many of these trains were made up to no less than 10 coaches, and loads such as these often caused problems for the small Stirling 0-4-4 tank locomotives which initially operated these heavy trains. It was not unknown for a Bradford-bound train to have exhausted the contents of the 1,000gal capacity side tanks by the time Laisterdyke station was reached! The G3 class 0-4-4 locomotives had a long association with the West Riding — 10 were delivered new from 1881, and the remaining six were transferred from the London area at the end of the century, but such services demanded somewhat more powerful machinery, and some of Ivatt's C2 4-4-2 tank engines were quickly despatched. The best motive power ever used on the service was the series of GNR/LNER 0-6-2 tank engines, and this era began in 1912 when four of Ivatt's powerful N1 class machines arrived. This advent certainly did not consign whole classes of elderly locomotives to the breaker's yard — the stopping trains continued to be operated by a mixture of Stirling 0-4-2 and 2-4-0 locomotives, Ivatt 4-4-0 and 0-4-4 side and well-tank engines and the occasional 0-6-0 goods engine. By 1909 tramway competition had made considerable headway and the 10-coach trains had been reduced to five or six vehicles, well within the capability of the older locomotives.

Leeds (Central) station had nine lines and seven platforms, the last two bays being completed in 1904. A great deal of shunting of passenger and goods trains was necessary in the approach area, and two signalboxes, A and B with 84 and 65 levers respectively, were used to control these movements. Staffing of the station was a joint GNR and LYR venture, with 130 people being employed by 1909. The dingy, smoke-filled shed witnessed 123 arrivals and 114 departures every 24hr, mostly concentrated between 03.34, with the arrival of the 22.45 from King's Cross, and 23.18, when the last local train for Bradford departed. By 1909 Leeds Central was served by nine up and eight down King's Cross expresses, with 13 of the total having refreshment cars. Bradford Exchange had seven trains each way daily, and the West Riding services gave a total of 10 connections daily on to the LYR system at Wakefield Kirkgate. The Leeds service played an historical part in the introduction of railway dining facilities when the first dining cars were introduced in 1879, to be followed by a regular service from the following year. The joint GNR/NER curve down to the MR and NER lines via Gelderd Junction was used almost entirely for excursion traffic operated by the GNR, NER, GCR, LNWR and LYR — the awkward reversal required at either Wortley Junction or Armley Junction precluded the curve's use by regular traffic. Separate GNR and LYR booking offices were provided at the station, but the LYR's busiest trade was in running summer excursions to Blackpool. Bradford Exchange also sported two booking offices, but here the LYR — who, of course, built the terminus and the entry from Low Moor — had a better share of the cake. By 1914 GNR and LYR trains were using all the

Right:
King's Cross 'A4' Pacific No 60003 *Andrew K. McCosh* slips on the start from Leeds (Central) with an express in the early 1960s.
Ian Allan Library

Below:
Fairburn Class '4' 2-6-4T No 42073 pauses between shunting duties at Central station during a snowstorm on 2 April 1966. *R. E. B. Siviter*

Bottom:
During the last days of steam haulage to King's Cross, 'A1' Pacific No 60148 *Aboyeur* approaches Holbeck High Level with the 09.42 up express from Central on 14 May 1963. *J. S. Whiteley*

platforms of the station and not sticking strictly to their own sides. The GNR's principal traffic lay along the route to King's Cross, and the LYR ran expresses to Manchester, Liverpool, Southport and Blackpool, with summer excursion traffic reaching Bridlington and Scarborough via the Calder Valley, Normanton and the NER. As well as having separate booking offices, the two companies also maintained their own parcels offices at Exchange station, but the adjacent Victoria Hotel was a GNR property. The fastest train to King's Cross took 3hr 56min for the 192½-mile journey, compared to the 3hr 25min required by the quickest train from Leeds which only had 185¾ miles to cover. After completion of the GCR main line, Sam Fay had tried to start a Leeds Central-Marylebone service, but the GNR would have none of it and quickly forbade the use of Central station for such a purpose! Although the route would have been about 19 miles longer than by the GNR line, the GCR was using the potential of its new line to the full and would certainly have rivalled the GN for speed south of Sheffield.

By the turn of the century Leeds New station had become one of the principal railway establishments in the country. Through Liverpool-Newcastle services had ended the practice of NER and LNWR staff keeping to their own station areas, and the NER was the dominant partner. The company had five exits (Wetherby, Selby, York, Castleford, Harrogate) compared to the LNWR's single entry from Manchester. NER trains in 1904 could reach Scarborough or Bridlington in 75min, or Newcastle (97 miles via Thirsk) in 2hr 28min, or 2hr 13min via York (106 miles). Hull (51 miles), Sunderland (90½ miles) and Middlesbrough (67½ miles) were reached in 70min, 124min and 127min respectively. The NER also ran through trains to Edinburgh and Glasgow in competition with the MR, and this service quickly became famous for high-speed running between Leeds, York and Newcastle. In 1914 the 08.55 departure from Leeds reached Edinburgh at 13.32 including stops at York and Newcastle. This was the fastest train to Edinburgh, and the breakfast and luncheon car express became known in later years as the 'North Briton'. Through carriages for Scarborough were detached at York in the winter-time, but these were deleted and replaced by a separate train in summer. The 08.55 was extended through to Glasgow from 19.10, from where the return train departed at 17.00. A further Edinburgh train left Leeds at 09.40 to travel via Harrogate and in the later NER years this train was retimed to depart at

09.10 to give some relief to the earlier departure. NER trains could reach Harrogate from either end of Leeds New station, a feature which must have been extremely useful in dealing with the heavy residential traffic to Harrogate and York (excursion traffic to the Yorkshire coast was heavy, and other summer traffic included workings between Scarborough and Bradford, Manchester and Liverpool). The branch from Cross Gates to Wetherby, on the Church Fenton-Harrogate line, was opened on 1 May 1876 as a single-line branch, and was doubled and modified slightly at the Wetherby end by 1902. This then allowed the NER to enter Leeds from the Marsh Lane direction, over their own line, and so avoid using the congested section from Canal Junction (where the outlets from New and Wellington stations met) to Holbeck. More importantly, it avoided the need for reversal in Leeds for the Liverpool-Hull/Newcastle trains.

Stations at Holbeck

Today nothing remains of the two stations which once existed at Holbeck, but for many years the location was the scene of never-ending railway activity. The High Level station was a joint GNR/LYR establishment placed on the exit from Central station at a point directly above the MR Leeds-Bradford line. The station was staffed by a GNR stationmaster who in 1902 had no less than 44 employees under his command, and the facilities were generally held to be 'comfortable and commodious'. Life at the Low Level station, however, was very different. This was a joint MR/NER station staffed by 14 men under the authority of the MR stationmaster and, such was the lack of service and high level of discomfort, that it was entered in a competition (around the year 1900) to find the most uncomfortable station in the country — which it won by a clear head! Two up and two down lines passed through the station, and the rough wooden uncovered platforms — all two of them — were barely 5ft wide. Winter conditions were particularly bad, when large numbers of wet or frozen passengers would have to fight their way along the wet and slippery boards to catch their train to Harrogate or Bradford. A waiting room on the 'departure' platform (for down trains) held 12 people within its 7ft×14ft confines, whilst the similarly-sized Ladies' Room was adorned with a mirror and travel information for those who wished to go on to either the United States or the Upper Nile! Traffic through the two stations in 1902 was indeed endless, and should have provided an unrivalled opportunity for exchange traffic. The High Level

station saw no less than 258 trains daily in summer, and the Low Level saw 220, including 120 stoppers and 46 NER trains. Obviously, not all these trains did stop at Holbeck, but the potential existed. Apart from the primeval condition of Low Level station, the natural events of railway development had conspired against Holbeck's further development. The MR originally used the station for passengers travelling to Harrogate — they could de-train at Low Level and catch a NER train via Bramhope. The development of New station and the Wetherby line made this an unnecessary change, as travellers could easily go on to the NER, and have the choice of route to Harrogate, from New station. Passengers between Harrogate and Bradford were originally routed via Low Level, but the start of regular, direct Harrogate-Otley-Bradford workings put an end to this circuitous route. Even more long-winded were the original Ilkley-Skipton and Ilkley-Bradford trains, which also reversed at Holbeck until the Guiseley Junction-Esholt Junction line opened in 1876 and the direct Ilkley-Skipton route was opened by the MR in 1888. The chaotic state of the Canal Junction-Whitehall Junction section made any connection involving the Harrogate line an extremely hazardous affair — many passengers missed a MR train to the south while it was held at signals at Whitehall Junction and the GNR sent one Harrogate express (the 13.30 from King's Cross) direct via York in order to avoid reversal out of Central on to the NER at Armley. The LNWR and LYR did persevere, and both ran Harrogate-Manchester services for some time which involved reversal at Central (for the LYR) or New (LNWR) stations. As previously mentioned, the NER were glad of their Wetherby route — it was a well-laid route, almost level, and allowed a good turn of speed for the 35min journey. Travellers on the GNR may have been tempted to change at High Level and continue to Harrogate via the NER, so saving a journey between the city's two main line stations, but the inconvenience outweighed the saving of a short cab fare. Such was the delay that many travellers probably made successive journeys from St Pancras instead of King's Cross, whence a simple change of platform at Wellington station was all that was required.

Early Trans-Pennine Services

The LNWR Leeds-Manchester route was the most crowded railway line in the country during the early years of the century. Despite the LNWR main line being many miles away, thus cutting the company out of any traffic destined for London or Scotland, the trans-Pennine expresses were amongst the LNWR's finest services, and they made no secret of being fully committed to maintaining a complete hold over the entire Leeds-Manchester run, expresses and stoppers alike. In 1904 the 43-mile journey was completed in 60min by the fastest trains, but the many smaller towns en route were fully served by the slower trains throughout the day. The 'New Line' was originally intended primarily for local trains, but congestion quickly demanded that some faster traffic should traverse the hilly and twisting route between Farnley and Heaton Lodge. By 1908 cheap return tickets were available by this route, and the return fares of 2s 9d (14½p) from Leeds to Manchester and 3s 3d (16p) to Liverpool generated some very heavy bookings. The

Leeds and Huddersfield service had no less than 19 non-stop trains daily each way (the fastest was the 10.10 ex-Leeds, taking just 19min, plus other trains which only stopped at Batley and Dewsbury. Some of these services were provided by the LNWR's through carriages from Leeds to South Wales and the southwest. In 1904 one portion ran daily to Birmingham, Bristol and Cardiff, but by 1908 the number had increased to three trains daily.

On the trans-Pennine run the Liverpool-Newcastle trains were made up of LNWR and NER stock and the Hull train entirely of LNWR vehicles. At New station the LNWR used Platforms 1 to 4, the NER used Platforms 5 to 10 and the through expresses used Platforms 5, 6 and 7. The Hull service was the pride of the LNWR in Yorkshire, and totalled five trains each way daily by 1908. Liverpool's first departure was at 11.00, and this train paused at Leeds between 13.12 and 13.25. Further stops were made at Selby and Staddlethorpe (since renamed Gilberdyke) before arriving in Hull at 14.34. This train often loaded to 19 vehicles, and must have demanded some extremely hard work from the locomotive and crew. The return working left Hull at 16.03 and paused in Leeds between 17.12 and 17.30. A corresponding working lcft Hull at 09.30 and reached Liverpool by 12.40, returning at 16.00 and reaching Hull at 19.27. These two workings were the duty of Leeds 'Precursor' class 4-4-0s, one of which was stationed at Hull for the workings. The day's last Hull-Liverpool train was made up of NER stock and was worked by a NER loco to Leeds. On the Newcastle service, speeds north of Leeds generally did not equal the NER's efforts on the Edinburgh trains or those of the LNWR

Hull trains — the fastest train from Liverpool was the 18.00 departure which arrived in Leeds at 19.53. Undoubtedly the NER felt that towns such as Harrogate, Northallerton and Darlington, and the great cathedral cities of York, Ripon and Durham, could not be deprived of good services merely for the sake of out-and-out speed. Between Leeds and Manchester speeds fell slightly by 1908, with the fastest trains — the 10.42 from Leeds and the 18.45 from Manchester — being allowed 68min including 3min at Huddersfield. The first departure from Leeds left at 06.00 and the last at 22.35. The last train was destined to become an extremely long-lived working, lasting well into diesel days as the 22.42 Leeds (ex-York)-Swansea mail. In LNWR days departure took place at 22.35 hauled, of course, by a Leeds 'Precursor' 4-4-0. Farnley Junction shed provided the motive power for these duties, originally powered mainly by 'Jumbo' 2-4-0s. As train loads increased the more powerful 4-4-0 classes took over — 'Benbow', 'Alfred the Great' and 'Precedent' types all appearing. The older four-cylinder compounds could hardly manage such a task, and even a 'Precedent' would be piloted with any more than nine bogies. Larger 'Experiment' 4-6-0s were rarely seen, except on excursion traffic or fast goods trains. As the LNWR was well known for thrashing the last possible unit of work out of even their most elderly locomotives, it is perhaps not surprising that even the occasional class 'DX' 0-6-0 goods engine turned up on passenger trains across the Pennines — usually a connection to South Wales or the West of England. The Leeds locomotives were dedicated to the trans-Pennine workings and never strayed on to the LNWR main line. Liverpool 'Precursors' often appeared, but locos from Manchester only appeared on slower trains. Excursion and holiday traffic was quite heavy, especially to North Wales, and in the years to 1914 the LNWR was regularly running a service of emigrant specials from Hull to Liverpool. Of the thousands of people driven from their European homelands at this time — from the Baltic, Russia and Poland — many crossed the North Sea en route to the United States, and the LNWR carried these sad cargoes to Liverpool for embarkation across the Atlantic. Some could not face the 3,000-mile sea voyage and left the trains to take their chances in Leeds, Bradford and Manchester instead.

By 1922 the principal through expresses totalled six trains daily eastwards, two each going to Newcastle, Hull or terminating at Leeds, and five westward trains with three from Hull and two from Newcastle. One of the Newcastle trains in each direction — the 14.10 from Liverpool and the 10.00 from Newcastle — conveyed through carriages between Leeds and Llandudno on Mondays and Fridays only during the summer months. But the rapid journeys of the pre-1914 era had gone, with the fastest trains taking 79min from Manchester to Leeds with a 4min pause at Huddersfield, and 82min in the reverse direction with a similar stop. The LNWR absorbed the LYR during 1922, but the LYR pattern of service from Liverpool and Manchester eastwards across the Pennines remained largely unaltered. The LYR main line ran along the Calder Valley to Wakefield and Goole, with

Leeds and Bradford being very much placed on separate byways. Nevertheless, the two cities were by this time well served with LYR trains to Manchester, Liverpool and Blackpool, whereas the company's trains between Manchester, York, Newcastle and Hull made no provision for Leeds or Bradford passengers. The LYR main line did not lend itself to providing competition against the might of the LNWR/NER services between Leeds, Bradford and Liverpool — a daily total of six westbound and seven eastbound trains were run, with three of the eastbound ones dividing at Halifax to serve the two cities and four trains going direct to Leeds but pausing at Low Moor for Bradford passengers to connect into the local service to Exchange station. These Leeds trains ran from Low Moor via Bowling and Laisterdyke, and at least one train called at Stanningley. All trains paused at Holbeck High Level and one train — the 16.35 from Liverpool — carried restaurant cars for both Leeds and Bradford portions. In the westbound direction four trains were combined from separate portions at Halifax, with the 09.15 Leeds/09.40 Bradford departure also including a slip coach for Rochdale. The following departure, the 13.02 Leeds/13.10 Bradford, was a vestibuled luncheon car train during weekdays, but on Saturdays the train ran simply as a Leeds-Southport working without any refreshments and with a connection at Low Moor. Only two trains ran direct from Leeds to Liverpool, the 07.53 and 15.50 departures, with the former calling at Stanningley.

The Calder Valley trans-Pennine service saw one train daily each way between Liverpool

and Newcastle during 1922. Both carried dining cars, and the westbound train also had a through carriage from Hull attached at Wakefield. Hull was reached from the west by a carriage detached from the 10.05 Manchester Victoria-Scarborough whose return working left Scarborough at 14.45 for arrival in Manchester at 18.05. The Manchester-Wakefield-Normanton-York trains totalled three eastbound and four westbound daily, with the 15.50 from Manchester carrying a slip portion for Todmorden and Burnley, and the eastbound trains being supplemented by a solitary working from Liverpool at 18.35. Two trains ran from Manchester to Bradford and three returned, and one train daily ran each way between Bradford and Liverpool.

Services to Hull were provided principally to connect with the Zeebrugge steamers. A daily departure from Liverpool at 14.00 ran to Hull Paragon and on Wednesdays and Saturdays this was advertised as a through Continental Boat Train, reaching Hull (Riverside) at 17.28, complete with through carriages from Preston and Burnley. The corresponding return train left Riverside on Tuesdays and Saturdays (departure was from Paragon on the remaining weekdays) at 08.45, also with a Preston portion. Another boat train service ran between Leeds, Bradford and Fleetwood, but only the westbound train was specifically advertised as a boat train. This left Leeds at 19.15 and joined the Bradford portion at Halifax, continuing thence with restaurant cars via Manchester instead of Burnley. The return working followed the same route but did not split, a 5min connection being made at

Low Moor for the benefit of the Bradford passengers whilst the breakfast-car train continued to Leeds for arrival at Central station at 09.58. On Mondays the train started from Manchester at 08.20, the Fleetwood run being curtailed presumably due to no steamers arriving from Belfast.

Goods Depots

The industrial establishments of Leeds and Bradford demanded the usual facilities for the supply of raw materials and fuel and the means of delivering the finished products to all parts of the country. Goods depots satisfied all these needs and also reflected the particular demands of the two cities. Bradford's wool trade was well catered for by the MR at Canal Road, the LYR at Bridge Street and the GNR at Adolphus Street. The MR establishment was next door to the Conditioning House, where wool and woollen goods were tested, and lay in a central part of the town where easy, level access was available for many miles with the minimum use of local horse transport. The LYR Bridge Street depot was also centrally placed but had the advantage of being subjected to much rebuilding and refitting at the time of the Exchange station rebuilding. Consequently it was a well-equipped depot, particularly in regard to the use of electric cranes and hoists, and handled vast amounts of wool brought in by the LYR, not just from local areas but also from the docks at Hull and Goole. Adolphus Street still suffered from being too far out of the city centre, but it was the GNR's principal goods terminal in Brad-

Far left:
Fairburn 2-6-4T No 42152 climbs out of Bradford with the 10.20 through coaches for King's Cross on 1 October 1967, the last day of steam haulage on these workings. The train has just passed Hammerton Street, and the Adolphus Street goods depot can clearly be seen in the background. *J. B. Mounsey*

Left:
A freight from Neville Hill reaches Beeston Junction behind 'J50' 0-6-0T No 68915 on 9 May 1959. *D. Butterfield*

Above:
Neville Hill West Junction today, looking towards Crossgates. *S. R. Batty*

ford and did handle part of the company's share of the woollen market (City Road and Manchester Road depots, off the Queensbury line, handled lesser amounts of traffic but were better situated for the town centre). Adolphus Street was adjacent to the city's produce and livestock markets, and the GNR carried large loads of perishable goods and cattle for this trade. Coal was carried in large quantities, especially to the electricity works at Valley Road (by the MR) and to the gas works at Planetrees Road, between Laisterdyke and Hammerton Street alongside the GNR line. Supplying coal, ore and limestone to the ironworks at Low Moor was a joint MR and GNR effort involving the Shipley-Laisterdyke branch as previously mentioned — the LYR approaches via Halifax or Mirfield must have

been much simpler. The MR's goods premises (including a bonded warehouse) were all located together in the Canal Road and Valley Road area, apparently for the exclusive use of the Midland, although it would seem likely that the NER would have been accommodated somewhere in the premises. The GCR ran services to the GNR's City Road and Adolphus Street depots, and the LNWR were accommodated at Manchester Road, Bridge Street and Vicar Lane, the latter being a LYR depot near Mill Lane Junction.

Although industrial Leeds had first grown up around the woollen trade, by 1914 this had been all but replaced by the clothing and engineering industries. Bradford's world dominance in wool was matched by the eclipse of the business in Leeds, and by the corresponding rise of tailoring and all forms of heavy engineering — particularly locomotives, printing machinery and foundry work. The principal depots were at Hunslet and Wellington Street, with others at Marsh Lane and

Cardigan Road and also with sidings into the larger works such as the Monk Bridge iron and steelworks and the corporation's great gasworks at New Wortley. Hunslet (Balm Lane) was built near the site of the original terminus of the NMR, by this time buried amidst the centre of the city's heavy engineering industry. A little further to the east, a new freight-only line was built across Hunslet Carr in 1899. This ran from Beeston Junction, on the GNR Wakefield line, to a new goods depot just to the east of the River Aire and the Aire & Calder Navigation. This depot was built alongside a new NER establishment reached by a short branch from the Leeds-Micklefield line at Neville Hill West Junction and a connection was made between the two systems at Hunslet. Through running was not readily achieved as reversals were involved in either direction — the prime object of both companies was to tap the heavy engineering factories of the area. The NER branch was granted an Act of Parliament in June 1893 (one month before the GNR line) and opened in January 1899, six months before the Beeston branch. This latter was originally promoted as the independent Hunslet Railway before being swallowed by the GNR in 1894. The NER branch contained nothing more exciting than a steep cutting within its 1½-mile length, but the GNR branch, of nearly four miles, had several bridges including one across the canal which was readily convertible into a swing bridge. Plans existed at the time to bring a ship canal into Leeds and the GNR had to bridge the

waterway accordingly. The expense to which the company was prepared to go indicates what a valued prize Hunslet must have been.

The Wellington Street area between Central station and Bean Ing Mill — the site of today's Yorkshire Post building — housed the depots of the NER, GNR, LNWR and LYR. Largest of these was the NER goods shed and grain warehouse and, despite having their Hunslet depot in much closer proximity to the various Leeds locomotive builders, this depot handled a greater annual tonnage of agricultural engines and equipment than any other on the NER. The LNWR and LYR shared a high-level goods shed and bonded warehouse and dealt with traffic reaching across the country from the Humber to Manchester, Fleetwood, Liverpool and Ireland. The GNR depot was sandwiched between these two, and shared access across the river from Gelderd Junction with the NER. The LNWR/LYR depot was approached from Holbeck by diverging tracks from the entrance to Central station. Despite Leeds being at one extreme, geographically speaking, of the NER system, the city was well catered for with plenty of sidings into the larger works — such as the Monk Bridge ironworks already mentioned. The original L&S terminus at Marsh Lane had been used as a goods depot since 1869, and dealt with express goods traffic to the northeast and Scotland. A small depot was opened in May 1900 at Cardigan Road in Burley, just off the Harrogate line, and this was destined to survive in use until 1972.

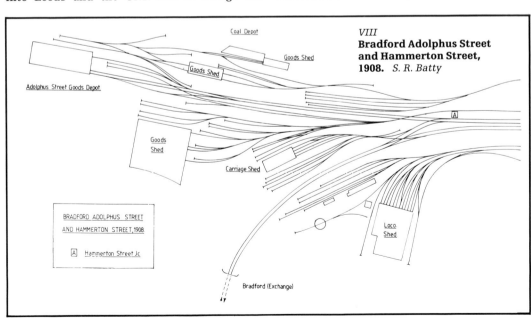

VIII
Bradford Adolphus Street and Hammerton Street, 1908. *S. R. Batty*

5 Passenger Travel Developments

Early Rationalisation

The outbreak of World War 1 in 1914 brought to an end the heady, relatively prosperous years of all the pre-Grouping railway companies, and the West Riding of Yorkshire felt this cold chill of leaner times ahead in no uncertain fashion. Stations had been closed on occasion since the 1850s, either due to lack of use or, more usually, due to replacement by a better establishment close by. Shortage of passengers saw an end to Royal Gardens on the Leeds-Harrogate line in September 1857, and to Bowling on the LBHJR connection in Bradford during February 1895. Kirkstall Forge station saw its last passengers in August 1905, whilst Halton Dial expired in February 1864. Station renewals closed the original premises at Holbeck, on the MR and NER exit from Leeds, during 1862, at Hunslet in September 1873, and at Wyke (known as Pickle Bridge until 1882) in September 1896. Of these early closures, two are remarkable for the long periods during which goods services were maintained after the loss of the passenger services — Kirkstall Forge was finally closed, after a long-forgotten existence, in 1959 and Bowling goods depot clung on until 4 May 1964, nearly 70 years after initial closure.

Tramway competition had been the most serious threat since the early years of the 20th century, and even the war years of 1914-18 delivered very few serious blows to the local railway services. The Leeds-Low Moor-Thornhill-Dewsbury-Tingley-Leeds circulars were all withdrawn in August 1914, and Manchester Road station was closed to passengers on 31 December 1915 but survived as a goods depot until May 1963. Perhaps the biggest casualty was the 1893 line from Dudley Hill to Low Moor which, after the circulars were withdrawn, was completely closed in 1916. One track was lifted immediately and, it is thought, was then reused by the army in France. The remaining track was left in to serve the GNR goods depot and this was not removed until after 1923, but the depot remained and is still in use today by a small industrial concern. Severe cuts were made nationwide in 1917, but only the Batley-Birstall branch of the LNWR suffered here with Carlinghow and Birstall stations closing from 1 January. Bailiff Bridge station was destroyed by fire in April 1917 and was not rebuilt. Gildersome East was a very remote station on the Leeds New Line, which was partially closed in January 1917 but rather oddly was reopened in March 1920. The station was well away from any sizeable population, especially Gildersome, and closure followed again in July 1921. Nevertheless both the LNWR and LMS must have had faith in the goods traffic — which had always played an important part in New Line affairs — for the ultimate closure did not take place until 30 September 1963. More competition followed from motorbuses, lorries and the start of private car ownership, but these effects had very little impact in terms of station closures during the years to 1939. Railway services were altered accordingly, using shorter trains, push-pull units and revised timetabling which whittled away many off-peak services.

The Cheap Day Return ticket — perhaps the most familiar feature of railway travel to generations of railway users and a much regretted casualty amidst today's plethora of confusing ticket schemes — was created during this period with the bus market firmly in mind. Co-operation with local road operators was not a feature of the Leeds and Bradford area as happened elsewhere, at Huddersfield, Sheffield or Todmorden. Perhaps the biggest casualty was the Shipley-Laisterdyke-Bradford Exchange passenger service, which ceased from 2 February 1931 with the closure to passengers of Shipley & Windhill, Thackley, Idle, and Eccleshill stations. Only Thackley closed completely, with Eccleshill surviving as a goods depot until November 1964 and the remaining two stations lasting until October 1968, the final stretch of the route, Laisterdyke to the English Electric factory at Bradford Moor, being removed in 1982. Dewsbury (Market Place)

Above:
The 1938-built Wellington station on the left appears to be in much better shape than the adjacent New station platforms in this early 1960s view. *Leeds City Libraries*

station, the LYR backwater branch of 1867, closed its gates to passengers in December 1930 but handled goods traffic for a further 30 years. Another ex-LYR casualty was Brighouse (Clifton Road), which closed completely on 14 September 1931. Hostilities from 1939 to 1945 once again left the railway network utterly exhausted, as in 1918, with a bleak future ahead. Only three closures took place and the strains of the war effort cannot have had any bearing on their futures. The stations were Woodkirk, on the ex-GNR Batley-Tingley line, closed on 25 September 1939, Churwell (between Leeds and Morley, on the ex-LNW line) 2 December 1940, and Flushdyke on the ex-GNR Wakefield-Dewsbury line which closed on 5 May 1941. One highlight of the interwar years was the rebuilding of Leeds (New and Wellington) stations into something more akin to a single station. Known as Leeds (City) from 2 May 1938, the rebuilding was a joint LMSR/LNER exercise which resulted in the former Wellington station being renamed Leeds City (North) and the original New station becoming Leeds City (South). Not surprisingly, this differentiation merely served to prolong the original identities of the separate stations, and the more general title of Leeds (City) was

quickly adopted. A new circulating area, offices and passenger facilities at the former Wellington station were the principal changes, together with a brand-new Queens Hotel which made an impressive appearance over City Square. So much space was taken by the new hotel that the two entrances to the station were rather cramped and inadequate, certainly in appearance, and did not do justice to the lofty, spacious area contained within. Alterations at New station were very small by comparison, indeed passengers probably saw no differences at all. The LNER North Eastern area undertook the improvement works, which consisted of resignalling the entire station from east to west. Leeds East box was converted to colour-light signalling from 3 March 1936 and similar work was completed at the West box by 4 April 1937. Leeds West's colour lights reached only as far as the LMSR

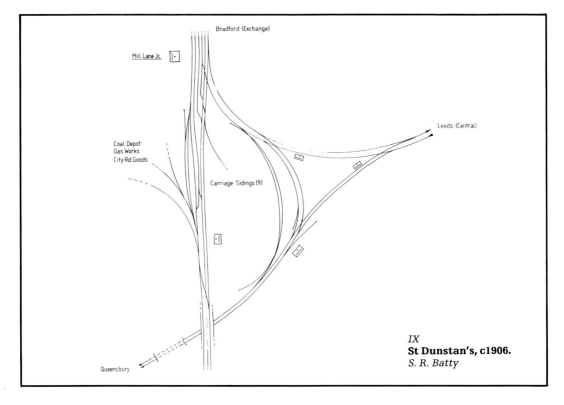

IX
St Dunstan's, c1906.
S. R. Batty

area covered by Leeds Junction box, which remained as a semaphore system.

Several famous named trains have served Leeds and Bradford, and the names generally originated either in the 1920s or 1940s. Most, but not all, of the titles were given to services connecting either or both of the cities to the capital, and the stories of these trains make an interesting chapter in the West Riding's railway history.

The Pullmans

Three Pullman trains have served King's Cross, Leeds and Bradford at various periods from 1923 to the present day. These are the 'Harrogate Pullman' (later the 'Queen of Scots') the 'West Riding Pullman' (later the 'Yorkshire Pullman') and, very briefly, the 'White Rose'.

At the Grouping of 1923 the LNER found itself with quite a lengthy period still unexpired on a Great Eastern Railway (GER) agreement with the Pullman Co. The GER had used the cars on their system with varying degrees of success or failure, and the new management decided that a Pullman train would be far more profitably employed running from King's Cross to Leeds, Harrogate and Newcastle. Accordingly, the 'Harrogate Pullman' started running in the summer of

1923, with the up train leaving Harrogate simultaneously with the down departure from London at 11.15, and both trains running non-stop between Leeds and London in 3hr 25min — then the best time to date. Two years later the train was extended to Edinburgh — still titled the 'Harrogate Pullman' — and the up Leeds departure was altered to 13.40. At this point the 'West Riding Pullman' was inaugurated, and the routes of the two trains became linked together. The Harrogate train was diverted away from Leeds, reaching Harrogate non-stop via Knottingley, Ferrybridge, Church Fenton and Tadcaster, and leaving the new Pullman to cater for Leeds. In 1928 the train was re-equipped with new stock, retitled the 'Queen of Scots', diverted back to Leeds in the path of the 'West Riding Pullman' and also extended to run through to Glasgow. The departure time had been altered from the original 11.15 to 11.20 in 1925, but was now put back to 11.15 again. Leeds was reached in 3hr 25min non-stop once more, and the Glasgow terminus was reached at 20.45 after a 480-mile journey. The up train left Glasgow at 10.05 and reached King's Cross at 19.35. The 'Queen' was certainly a successful train and ran until the outbreak of war in 1939, by which date the time taken between

Leeds and London, up and down, had been reduced to 3hr 11min.

Restoration of this service took place in 1952, but the train was now made up of 10 cars equal to about 400 tons, considerably heavier than the lightweight 290-ton train of 1939. Larger motive power was needed, and the new 'A1' and 'A2' Pacifics took over from the powerful Ivatt Atlantics between London and Leeds. After an early unsuccessful period of haulage by ex-GCR class 'B3' 4-6-0s, the 'Queen of Scots' was hauled over this southern section of its journey either by ex-GCR 'Director' 4-4-0s based at Copley Hill, or by King's Cross Atlantics. The 'Directors' were fine machines, which were paired with the Leeds men to give some dazzling performances, but the boiler power and ease of running of the Class 'C1' 4-4-2s produced feats of acceleration and hard running which were only bettered by the much larger Pacific fleet introduced from 1937. Some performances all but matched those of the LNER streamlined trains of the later 1930s, with the best work being done after the Leeds 'Directors' were replaced by Atlantics in 1932.

But back to the 1950s. Steam haulage continued until the advent of the 'Deltic' era, but the 'Queen' was not destined to enjoy the benefits of high speed for very long. In the summer of 1964 the train was cut back to serve Harrogate only, with a Bradford portion going on from Leeds Central. At the same time the title was abandoned and replaced by the 'White Rose' headboard, as obviously the train had lost all pretention to any Scottish connection.

The 'West Riding Pullman' started running in September 1925, using Pullman stock which the LNER had unsuccessfully tried to operate between King's Cross, Sheffield and Manchester. Departure from London was at 11.10, 10min ahead of the 'Queen', and the train ran non-stop to Leeds in 3hr 25min, again involving some fine work from the Atlantics. Two cars went on to Bradford and the rest of the train was worked as empty stock to Harrogate, where departure on the following day took place at 11.15; the Bradford portion left at 11.20 and the combined train left Central station at 11.50 for arrival at King's Cross at 15.15. By virtue of the ECS working, Harrogate was graced with two up Pullman trains daily, but only one down arrival.

Major changes were made when the 'Queen of Scots' was diverted back to serve Leeds in

Left:
The second (1873) station at Hunslet, two days before closure on 13 June 1960.
G. C. Lewthwaite

Below:
Ivatt 'Atlantics' produced some magnificent work between Leeds and King's Cross, not least with the 'Queen of Scots' Pullman. No 3280 is seen here at Copley Hill shed, complete with headboard, on 21 July 1935.
W. L. Good

1928. The 'West Riding Pullman' departure from London was moved to 16.45 and the train was extended to run on to Newcastle. Two years earlier a stop had been inserted at Wakefield, where a portion was detached for Bradford and Halifax. This left Westgate station and travelled via Morley to Bradford Exchange, departing thence for Queensbury and reaching Halifax within 4hr 15min of the London departure. More changes followed in the mid-1930s with the introduction of the streamlined trains. In 1935 the 'Silver Jubilee' rendered the Pullman's Newcastle portion obsolete, and this was replaced by a Hull section which was attached and detached at Doncaster. As the train was now firmly rooted within Yorkshire, the name was changed to 'Yorkshire Pullman' — presumably the geographical difficulties had precluded such a change being made in 1928! In 1937 the streamlined 'West Riding Limited' began

running to Leeds and Bradford, with the up train departing in the middle of the morning — almost exactly in the Pullman's spot. To avoid competing with the 'Limited' the Leeds and Bradford departures of the Pullman were abandoned, and the Harrogate and Halifax portions were combined at Doncaster with the cars from Hull. The Harrogate cars travelled via Knaresborough and York, whilst the Halifax cars were worked in as empty stock, presumably via Queensbury, Laisterdyke and Wakefield. The down train left King's Cross at 16.45, well ahead of the 'Limited', and carried the normal portions for Leeds and Halifax.

After being abandoned during the war the train was restored from 4 November 1946. The down departure was altered to 17.30 in 1949, giving a 3hr 46min journey to Leeds and, as the streamlined trains were not resumed, up departures were made from Bradford at 10.15 and Leeds at 10.45. Harrogate departure was at 10.07, but the Halifax extension was gone for good. The 1950s passed the train without note, but the year 1961 saw the down train become an early recipient of 'Deltic' motive power, a change which instantly lopped almost 40min off the time to Leeds. Full 'Deltic' working did not come until 1963 and by

Below:
The slender lines of the 'A3' Pacifics are shown to advantage in this view of No 60086 *Gainsborough* **slipping on the start out of Leeds (Central) with the 'Queen of Scots' in the late 1950s.** *E. Treacy*

1967, with the Hull portion withdrawn and the train running non-stop to Wakefield, Leeds was reached in 3hr 1min, Bradford in 3hr 37min and Harrogate in 3hr 44min. Locomotive haulage continued until the end of the 1977/78 timetable, when the train was abandoned as an anachronism amidst the high-speed train (HST) services then being introduced to Leeds and Bradford. Outdated or not, the 'Pullman' was covering the Leeds and London run inside 2hr 55min up and 2hr 52min down. Final departure times were 09.50 from Bradford, 10.30 from Leeds, 09.55 from Harrogate and 17.04 from King's Cross. Seven years lapsed before the train was reincarnated as a result of BR's InterCity Sector looking for some extra gloss to apply to their ECML services, and the Pullman name was revived and applied to the former 'Leeds Executive' which left City station at 07.30. Bradford passengers had to use a diesel multiple-unit (DMU) to reach Leeds, and the new 'Yorkshire Pullman' ran non-stop to King's Cross in 2hr 15min from 13 May 1985. The down train was slower, with stops at Grantham, Doncaster and Wakefield, but it also ran through to Bradford calling at New Pudsey. A Wakefield stop for the up train was made from the

following September, and the 1988 train leaves Leeds at 07.15, by popular demand, to give a London arrival time of 09.30.

The 'White Rose' qualifies as a Pullman working by virtue of the title being used on the remains of the 'Queen of Scots' train for the brief period from 1964 to 1967. Prior to this the train had run as a heavy working for Leeds and Bradford, with the name being applied in 1949. Historically, the train could claim origins which reached back to the GNR days before 1914, when a departure for Leeds left King's Cross at 09.45 and reached the city, non-stop to Doncaster, in 3hr 40min. The up train left at 17.30, and this departure time remained in force right up to 1939. In LNER days the King's Cross departure was altered to 10.10 and the train was split into portions for Hull, Bradford, Leeds and Harrogate, with the Hull portion being detached at Doncaster, the Bradford at Wakefield and the Harrogate

Below:
'A3' 4-6-2 No 60053 *Sansovino* climbs past Copley Hill MPD with the 12.45 to King's Cross in the early 1950s. Class 'N5' 0-6-2T No 69266 stands on the shed coal ramp line. *E. Treacy*

coaches being detached from the Leeds restaurant car at Central station and continuing via the former NER route via Arthington. These heavy trains often approached 500 tons gross weight and meant some hard work for the crews of the Ivatt Atlantics which were the principal source of power. Pacific haulage did not come until the later 1930s when Class 'A4' machines took over and eased the load, but the train was suspended in 1939 at the outbreak of World War 2. Ten years later the train reappeared as the 09.18 King's Cross-Doncaster-Leeds/Bradford, running non-stop to Doncaster and reaching Leeds by 13.11, with the up train leaving Central station at 17.15 for a 4½hr run. Speed was never to be a feature of the 'White Rose', although matters improved somewhat from 1958 when many stops south of Doncaster were cut out and the up train left Leeds at 15.35 and arrived in London at 19.18. 'Deltic' performance then gave a faster schedule between London and Doncaster, but when a real speed-up of ECML services took place in 1967 it was too late for the 'White Rose'. As mentioned previously, the train was turned over to Pullman operation in the summer of 1964, to work the remains of the former 'Queen of Scots' to Leeds and Harrogate, and the 'White Rose' Pullman ceased to run from March 1967. By this time the Leeds-London journey had been cut to only 2hr 55min, a far cry from the 4½hr of the 1949 timetable.

The 'West Riding Limited'

The LNER's famous streamlined expresses, the 'Silver Jubilee' and 'Coronation', commenced running non-stop to Newcastle in September 1935 and to Edinburgh in July 1937 respectively. Nigel Gresley had been interested in the work of a high-speed DMU which had been put into service in Germany, and decided that possibilities for such a train were present on the LNER. He even requested the builders to outline the design and performance of such a train for the ECML, but the resulting figures were disappointing and the idea was dropped. Nevertheless, Gresley knew that a high-speed train would undoubtedly be successful in commercial terms, and he also knew that the appeal of a high-speed steam-hauled train would be immeasurably greater than any interest generated by diesel or electric locomotion.

To assess the feasibility of high-speed steam haulage a test run was made in November 1934 from King's Cross to Leeds and back, using 'A1' Pacific No 4472 *Flying Scotsman* and a light-weight train of four coaches (147 tons) going down and of six coaches (208 tons) for the return. Leeds was reached in only 2hr 32min and the up journey was rattled off in 2hr 37min at a time when the fastest scheduled time was 3hr 10min, and this was achieved using a locomotive which the running staff felt was not one of the best Pacifics in service at the time! The streamliners duly entered service to Newcastle and Edinburgh, but the West Riding had to wait until September 1937 before receiving any benefit from the new trains. The 'West Riding Limited' was made up of eight articulated vehicles, as per earlier streamlined trains but without the beaver-tail observation car used on the 'Coronation', giving 48 first-class and 168 third-class seats, and the first train left Leeds Central at 11.33 on 27 September 1937 hauled by garter blue 'A4' Pacific No 4492 *Dominion of New Zealand*. Two 'A4' locomotives were indeed named specifically for the new train, Nos 4495 *Golden Fleece* and 4496 *Golden Shuttle*, but these were not completed at Doncaster Works in time to appear on the new train at inception. The first train left Leeds without any particular ceremony, and the arrival at King's Cross created no interest whatsoever — after all, streamliners had been around since 1935! Maximum speed was well over 90mph and the average was 69mph, all of which just about managed to impress a Leeds geologist who used the train — more by accident than design, one feels — as the first leg of his journey to Bombay!

The articulated train was hauled between Leeds and Bradford by a pair of N2 class 0-6-2 tank engines. Departure from Bradford was at 11.10, from Leeds at 11.33 and arrival in King's Cross was scheduled for 14.15. The down train left at 19.10 and reached Leeds at 21.53 and Bradford at 22.15, and these times brought Bradford within 3hr 5min of London whilst reducing the Leeds time to only 2hr 42min up and 2hr 43min down — times which would not be bettered for many years ahead. Like the 'Silver Jubilee' and the 'Coronation', the 'Limited' was a successful, well-used train which disappeared from the railway scene in 1939 and never reappeared. The coaching stock was put into store at Copley Hill, and languished there for several years until eventually part of the set was put back into service in 1949 on a new train called the 'West Riding' which left King's Cross at 15.45 for a non-stop run to Wakefield. A Bradford portion was left here, to travel via Morley, and the remainder terminated at Leeds Central. This train ran to Leeds in 3hr 53min, and the up train — the 07.50 from Leeds — needed no less

than 1min under 4hr for the journey. In 1960 the title of the down train was moved to an express which left King's Cross at various times between 07.45 and 08.00 over the succeeding years, and the name lapsed into obscurity with the launch of the 'Executive' trains of the 1970s.

The 'Yorkshireman' and 'South Yorkshireman'

These two trains connected Bradford Exchange directly with London, ie without calling at Leeds, and followed unique routes at the northern ends of their journeys. The 'Yorkshireman' was a LMSR creation of 1925, and the 'South Yorkshireman' was a very early BR title bestowed in 1948.

Before 1914 the MR, GCR and GNR had competed with each other for the London-Sheffield traffic and some very fast running had resulted. The MR had run between the two cities in 3hr 10min, but any further improvement was stopped in 1914. After the war the LMSR revived this fast Sheffield schedule for one train each way, which was extended to Bradford Exchange station by means of the Royston-Thornhill line and thence by using running powers over the former LYR from Thornhill Junction to Heckmondwike and Low Moor. The new train was called the 'Yorkshireman' and trains left Bradford at 09.10 and St Pancras at 16.55 for the 4hr 15min run. Some acceleration followed from 1937, when a Leicester stop was removed, and the time thereby reduced to 4hr 1min but, by 1939, this stop had been put back into the timetable and the journey lengthened to no less than 4hr 20min. The train was withdrawn in 1939 and never reinstated, as the Royston-Thornhill line lost all passenger traffic during the war years, before falling into total disuse.

The 'South Yorkshireman' was named by BR in 1948 and ran from Exchange station at 10.00 for an arrival at Marylebone station at 15.30, with the down train leaving at 16.50 for the 5½hr journey back to Bradford. Origins could be traced back to pre-Grouping days, when similar trains left Bradford at 10.00 and Marylebone at 18.20, but the BR trains were somewhat heavier and had extra stops included. In GCR days the train was usually worked between Bradford and Sheffield by a

LYR locomotive, often a Hughes four-cylinder 'Dreadnought' 4-6-0 but occasionally a locomotive of much humbler aspirations such as an 0-6-0 goods engine worked the service. This northern extremity of the train's route was particularly interesting. The up train would call at Low Moor and then proceed via the Spen Valley line on to the Calder Valley and so into Huddersfield; conditional stops were then made at Brockholes and Shepley before the train passed through Penistone, non-stop to Sheffield. In the down direction a pause was made at the latter place en route to Huddersfield, but the conditional stops were made at Heckmondwike, Liversedge and Cleckheaton before the final pause at Low Moor.

A naming ceremony was held at Bradford Exchange station in May 1948, attended by the Lord Mayors of Bradford and Huddersfield, four LNER coaches and two ex-GNR restaurant cars and ex-LMS Class '5' 4-6-0 No M5101 in the charge of Driver Tordoff and Fireman Lister. After the brief ceremony the short train departed from Platform 5, with banking assistance provided by ex-LYR 2-4-2T No 50909. Quite why such extra effort was required for a short train hauled by a modern locomotive such as No M5101 was not explained at the time! Alas, the 'South Yorkshireman' was not destined for either a long or illustrious career. The train was cancelled altogether during a fuel crisis in 1951, and afterwards the former GCR route to London commenced a period of steady decline whilst the ECML was gradually improved. The schedule could never compete with services offered via Leeds and Doncaster, and timekeeping was inconsistent at the London end of the route. Withdrawal of the train took place with the winter timetable of 1960, by which time the route to Marylebone had been reduced to little more than a long branch line.

The 'Executives'

The 'Executive' appendage has been applied to so many products and services in recent years that the term is now beginning to appear decidedly hackneyed wherever it is used — certainly the titles 'Leeds Executive', 'Bradford Executive' and 'West Yorkshire Executive' do not have the same pleasant ring as some of the more illustrious titles of past years. These services grew out of the accelerated services of the 1970s, and the Leeds and Bradford trains were titled as such in 1973. The 'Leeds Executive', with 'Deltic' haulage, finally restored the Leeds and London times to prewar standards in 1976 with up and down times of

Above:
The down 'North Briton' moves out of Leeds City
on 11 October 1958 behind 'A1' 4-6-2 No 60121
Silurian. *M. Mitchell*
148

Below:
Holbeck 'Royal Scot' 4-6-0 No 46145 *The Duke of
Wellington's Regiment (West Riding)* heads away
from Leeds (City) towards Carlisle with the down
'Thames-Clyde Express'. *E. Treacy*

2hr 43min, and 2hr 42min for the 07.30 Leeds and 15.55 King's Cross departures respectively. These times were further reduced to 2hr 28min and 2hr 26min respectively by the end of the 'Deltic' period in 1978, and the HST service which followed cut these times by 1982 to 2hr 7min and 2hr 10min, with the down train continuing to Harrogate. The departure time was altered to 16.50 and an extra stop was included at Wakefield, but the up train remained non-stop from Leeds to King's Cross and, for 1982 and 1983, the departure time was altered to 07.53. The revived 'Yorkshire Pullman' took over the path of the up train from May 1985, but the down service continued throughout the year until the name was finally abandoned in 1986.

Bradford joined the 'Executive' club in 1973 also, again with eight coaches hauled at high speed by a 'Deltic' locomotive. Use of the Wortley curve to avoid Leeds helped to ensure a run to King's Cross for the 07.36 train of 2hr 36min with stops at New Pudsey, Wakefield, Doncaster and Peterborough, although the latter was soon removed from the schedule. Going down, departure times in the pre-HST era varied between 15.45 and 15.55, without any Peterborough stop being included. Some strange events followed the introduction of HST services and, initially, the train showed no great improvement in timing as had happened to the Leeds train. For a short period the down train was not named and, in 1982, a Grantham stop was included also. The name was restored in 1983 at the same time as the down working was routed via Leeds and a further 17min added to the journey time. In the following year the up train was also re-routed and the Bradford departure was brought back from 07.36 to 07.18 in order to maintain a King's Cross arrival of 10.10. Naturally these events were not generally well received by the executive rail-users of Bradford, but the changes of 1986 were farther-reaching. The 07.18 up train was cancelled and replaced by an untitled departure at the early hour of 06.04 which reached King's Cross at 08.57. Admittedly this gave a better arrival for a day's work in the capital, but the journey time did not compare with those offered by similar trains arriving from Leeds or York. The down train departure was altered from 15.50 to 16.50, which also lengthened the available working day. During 1988 the up train was retitled and moved back to the 1985 timings, ie 07.18 from Bradford, and stops at Leeds, Wakefield, Doncaster and Peterborough before arriving at 10.13.

Last of the trio is the 'West Yorkshire Executive', a name which was bestowed in 1984 upon the 07.50 from King's Cross to Leeds and the 15.45 return train. Historically these trains are the modern counterparts of the old 'White Rose' workings, with about 2hr difference in running times. The down train is the faster of the two, taking 2hr 24min with stops at Stevenage, Peterborough and Wakefield, whilst the up working pauses at Wakefield, Doncaster, Newark and Peterborough and requires 2hr 29min for the journey.

The 'North Briton'

This train was a daily return working between Leeds and Edinburgh via Newcastle, extended and altered over a period of 70 years to serve Glasgow, Dundee and Aberdeen. The northbound train was much better patronised than the southbound one, probably due to the latter's late hour of arrival in Leeds. The MR route via Carlisle to Edinburgh was somewhat shorter than the NER/North British alternative, but the steep and difficult road via Ais Gill could not compare, in terms of speed, with the fast and level route via York, Darlington and Newcastle. The 08.50 Edinburgh departure from Leeds during the early years of the century involved some extremely fast running between York and Newcastle, and thence to Edinburgh by courtesy of the NBR. The experiences of the 1895 races to the north were obviously put to good use by the NER and NBR!

This train arrived in Edinburgh at 13.30 and then returned at 18.25 for a Leeds arrival of 23.45, and at that time was not named. The service was extended to Glasgow in 1910 and in 1914 the Leeds departure was delayed until 09.00, with arrival at Edinburgh at 13.32. During the postwar years the train became very heavy and yet had to rely on Gresley 'D49' class 4-4-0 power right through from Leeds to Newcastle, where 'A1'/'A3' Pacific power took over. By bringing forward the departure times of the up train and also by using Pacific locomotives all the way to York the arrival at Leeds was improved to 22.00 from the previous time of 23.45-midnight.

Naming took place in 1949 and, by 1952, this train — still loading to nearly 400 tons — was running at 63mph between Darlington and York. The pre-1939 schedule was regained with the down train leaving Leeds at 09.05 and reaching Edinburgh by 13.32. A pause of 18min preceded the departure for Glasgow, which was reached at 14.57 and where a turnaround of only 63min was allowed before return

Above:
The down 'Harrogate Pullman' arrives at Leeds (Central) behind Ivatt Atlantic No 1459 sometime during 1923/24, when the train ran to Harrogate via reversal at Central station.
W. H. Whitworth/Rail Archive Stephenson

departure took place. Edinburgh was left at 17.14 and Leeds arrival took place at 22.02. The 'North Briton' was an exclusive 'A3' job from Leeds until dieselisation was effected during the early 1960s. Dieselisation brought about an earlier start from Leeds at 08.40, arrival in Edinburgh at 12.51 and no run on to Glasgow. The up train was correspondingly faster, and both trains also called at Durham and Dunbar. The name disappeared briefly from 1968 to 1972 but, from 1972 to 1975, was applied to a train which ran from Leeds to Dundee and Aberdeen. Final disposal of the name came with the HST era, but shadows of the working have persisted since 1979 and even in 1988 there exist two HST workings which recall this famous name — the 07.00 Leeds-Edinburgh (arr 10.20) and 18.20 Aberdeen-Leeds (arr 00.13) via Edinburgh at 20.55.

The 'Thames-Clyde Express' and the 'Waverley'

These two expresses ran from St Pancras via the Midland main line to Leeds, thence via the Settle & Carlisle to Glasgow or Edinburgh. Both trains were named by the LMSR in 1927, although the latter train was initially known as the 'Thames-Forth Express'. The up and down 'Thames-Clyde' workings left Glasgow

St Enoch at 09.30 and St Pancras at 10.00 respectively, taking 8hr 55min and 8hr 38min for their journeys. The trains reversed at Leeds City, the down train at 13.44 and the up at 14.20, and the locomotives involved were invariably 'Jubilee' class 4-6-0s towards the war years. During the 1939-1945 period the train continued to run, but in very different circumstances. The restaurant cars were abandoned and replaced by an Edinburgh portion, and the whole train was regularly loaded to 14 vehicles which needed no less than 11½hr and 11¾hr respectively for the down and up journeys. These heavy trains were still 'Jubilee'-powered to Leeds, sometimes with assistance from a 4-4-0, but the hard climb to Ais Gill was usually done by a single 'Royal Scot' 4-6-0. After the war the Edinburgh portion was dropped, and the restaurant cars from St Pancras to Glasgow via the Settle & Carlisle line were abandoned.

The 'Waverley' followed a similar course through history, starting life in 1927 as the summer-only 'Thames-Forth Express' which left St Pancras at 09.05 and reversed in Leeds at 13.05 en route to Carlisle and Edinburgh. Fast running was needed as far as Nottingham, but from here to Leeds the pace was reduced by virtue of colliery workings, curves and the pull up to Bradway tunnel. Beyond Leeds the train was booked for a very fast run to Carlisle which meant that some very hard work was needed after the pause at Skipton, and which certainly allowed for no gentle recovery down the Eden Valley. Carlisle was reached at 15.14, and there the train was handed over to the LNER who worked it over the Waverley route via Hawick and Galashiels to Edinburgh, where for some years a connection was possible with the down 'Flying

Scotsman'! This route had some fearsome uphill sections, particularly at Whitrope and Falahill, but the 'A1' and 'A3' Pacifics were masters of the task and coped well with the gradients and intermediate stops from their introduction to the route in the late 1920s. The down train reached Waverley station at 17.45, 8hr 40min, from St Pancras, and the up train had an easier schedule of 9hr 17min after departing from Edinburgh at 10.03.

During the war years the train was discontinued and replaced by an Edinburgh portion attached to the 'Thames-Clyde Express'. The train was restored to service, but unnamed, from October 1945 with a non-stop Leeds-Carlisle run and an arrival at Edinburgh some 1½hr later than in prewar days. The southbound train took over 11¼hr to reach London until 1952, after which improvements were made to both trains which resulted in better schedules south of Nottingham. Renaming took place as late as 1957, when the original title was renounced in favour of the 'Waverley', a rather more descriptive name in view of the train's route beyond Carlisle. More useful was the much faster schedule given to the train — St Pancras was left at 09.15 for a non-stop run to Nottingham, and Carlisle was reached 40min earlier at 16.02, with journey's end at Edinburgh at 18.52. The up train left at 10.05 and reached St Pancras at 17.48, also considerably faster than over the past five years. During 1960 some ex-LNER 'A3' Pacifics were transferred to Holbeck shed for working between Leeds, Carlisle and Glasgow, and these machines distinguished themselves by giving some very impressive performances indeed over this difficult route.

Unfortunately the service was not well used and after a few years the 'Waverley' returned to a summer-only timetable, with an Edinburgh portion again being added to the 'Thames-Clyde Express'. During the winter months the St Pancras departure travelled only as far as Leeds and Bradford. Diesel haulage took over in much the same fashion and with virtually identical results to the pattern which was followed with the 'Thames-Clyde', ie with leisurely schedules more appropriate to a scenically-attractive railway than to any inter-city route. The diversion via Wakefield and Moorthorpe was instituted in 1967, by which time the up and down trains needed 9hr 15min for their journeys, and the last St Pancras-Edinburgh trains ran in the following year. This route could not offer any competition to the ECML in terms of sheer speed, and the line was closed and lifted in 1969.

The 'Cornishman'

If ever a case existed of a title looking for a train, it must surely apply to the 'Cornishman'. One hundred years ago it was bestowed upon a GWR Paddington-Penzance train which became the last broad gauge departure from London in May 1892. The train continued in

Below:
An unidentified 'Clan' Pacific passes Whitehall Junction with a northbound special in 1966.
L. A. Nixon

service until cast into oblivion by the fast, new 'Cornish Riviera Limited' during 1904. Revival came no less than 48 years later with a Wolverhampton-Penzance train running via Birmingham, Stratford and Cheltenham, but some years afterwards the Honeybourne-Cheltenham route was closed and the train was diverted to run along the former Midland line from Cheltenham to Birmingham. At this stage the train was extended on to Derby and Sheffield — and abandoned Wolverhampton altogether — and, later, was extended through to Leeds and Bradford via the Midland ex-L&BR route. From May 1967 the train left Bradford (Exchange) station and travelled to Sheffield via New Pudsey, Wakefield and the former S&K line, leaving Bradford at 07.06, Leeds at 07.36, and reaching Penzance by 17.55. The northbound train left Penzance at 11.00 and reached Leeds and Bradford at 21.31 and 22.07 respectively. The Bradford service was discontinued in 1971 and the title was removed from the Leeds train in 1975, and any resemblance to the original workings from Leeds and Bradford was lost with the introduction of HSTs on the upgraded northeast-southwest route from October 1981. True to its own peculiar knack for survival, however, the 'Cornishman' title reappeared in May 1987 on yet another service — the HST-operated 11.25 Newcastle-Penzance and corresponding 07.30 return, both of which travel between Sheffield and York via Doncaster and the ECML.

The 'Devonian'

This title was created in 1927 and applied to a train which had connected Bradford with Paignton for many years, although only a set of through carriages went all the way to Devonshire — the express working terminated at Bristol. The new train left Bradford Forster Square at 10.25 and reversed at Leeds City before making a 50min run to Sheffield. Some very fast running followed to Derby and Birmingham, but the three Paignton coaches were taken on from Bristol at a very leisurely pace by the GWR, and Paignton was not reached until 18.51. The northbound train left at 09.15 for the stroll to Bristol but fast work followed to Birmingham, and Leeds was reached at 17.24 and Forster Square at 17.54. During the summer months the entire train was worked through in both directions between Kingswear and Bradford. The train was a regular 'Jubilee' working over the LMSR system.

After being taken off during the war years

the train reappeared in October 1946, with schedules of 8¾hr to Torquay (compared to 8hr 26min in 1939) and 8hr 57min coming north (8hr 39min in 1939) and these times were increased to 9½hr-9¾hr during the 'austerity' years of the late 1940s. Acceleration came about in the 1950s and the use of double-headed 'Jubilee' power was frequently seen until the 'Peak' class diesels took over in the early 1960s.

From May 1967 the northern terminus was changed to Bradford Exchange and the train was diverted via Wakefield and Moorthorpe for the approach to Sheffield, and by this time the train was running throughout the year from Bradford to Paignton — after a period of running to and from Bristol only during the winter months — with dining facilities being conveyed to and from Leeds. Like many other Midland line services, the 'Devonian' schedule of the early 1970s was not much of an improvement over those of the late 1930s. The title was dropped in 1975 but the service was revived, after a fashion, with the northeast-southwest HST service of 1982 when a Bradford/Leeds-Paignton train was introduced with a total journey time of just 6hr 40min. An early departure of 06.15 was made and this continued, with some variation, until a change was made to 07.00 in October 1986. The northbound service introduced in 1982 was greatly altered in that the train left Leeds for Newcastle, so avoiding Bradford altogether. Bradford's southbound departure disappeared from the timetable in May 1987 when the train was cut back to depart from Leeds, so finally severing the city's connection with a through service to the southwest which dated back well over 60 years.

Ironically, the 'Devonian' title was restored at this time, and the train now leaves Leeds at 06.15 for a 5hr 43min run to Paignton, followed by a return departure at 12.38 which reaches Leeds at 18.27.

As is clear from these brief descriptions, many of these trains have origins which go back a long way before the actual name was given to the train. Any readers who are interested to learn more about these titles are recommended to read *Titled Trains of Great Britain* by B. K. Cooper (sixth edition), published by Ian Allan Ltd.

Right:
The southbound 'Devonian' climbs past St Dunstan's behind a BR/Sulzer 'Peak' in August 1970. *M. Dunnett*

6 The Postwar Years and the End of Steam

The Austerity Years

The end of six long dark years of war found the railways of Great Britain in a state of utter exhaustion, and the West Riding network was no exception to this general rule. Compared to many large cities the area had suffered relatively little bomb damage, but the railway's hardware, infrastructure, manpower and services were worn out. Years of overloading and lack of maintenance had taken their toll of the locomotive fleet, very many of which were well past their best years by 1939 anyway. Several modern designs — such as Stanier's Class '5' 4-6-0s, Class '8' 2-8-0s and Class '4' 2-6-4Ts, Gresley's 'V2' 2-6-2s and Pacifics, Thompson's 'B1' 4-6-0s — had the power and ruggedness needed to survive years of necessary abuse and lack of maintenance, but even these modern locomotives were in a far from perfect condition by 1946. The older classes had not fared as well, and many of these barely scraped past Nationalisation in 1948 before being condemned. Many did survive, however, and could face a future of perhaps 10 or 15 years before dieselisation finally sealed their fate. Similarly, the track-work, signalling, civil engineering and public works had all been severely overloaded and

badly neglected. Bradford's two terminal stations were in dire need of attention, especially Exchange station, but whereas Forster Square's overall roof was removed and replaced by a smaller set of modern metal and glass awnings during 1953, the former station was destined to be allowed to decay slowly until total demolition and replacement by a new building on a different site began during the early 1970s. The ex-MR station, known simply as 'Bradford' since reopening in 1890, had been renamed to the far more suitable 'Bradford Forster Square' on 2 June 1924, and this was the only significant change viewed by the travelling public for almost 30 years. Leeds Central remained as a smoky, dark little station which seemed far too squalid to handle main line expresses to and from King's Cross. City station remained as a stark contrast between the new Wellington platforms and the unaltered LNWR/NER platforms of 1879. Lastly, and most importantly, the people who made the railway work had suffered most of all. Years of long hours, under conditions now unheard of, with equipment which was often just one step from the scrapyard, had left their marks on a workforce which suddenly found that railway employment was no longer the

Bottom left:
A stopping train from Forster Square arrives at Leeds (City) behind well-presented Aspinall 2-4-2T No 50636 on 20 April 1954. *R. C. Hodge*

Left:
A credit to Starbeck's cleaners — 'D49/2' 4-4-0 No 62773 *The South Durham* **approaches Whitehall with a Harrogate train.**
Ian Allan Library

Bottom:
Class 'C12' 4-4-2T No 4535 at Copley Hill on 21 July 1935. These locomotives worked many local trains on the ex-GNR lines, but No 4535 was withdrawn in January 1939. *W. L. Good*

highly-esteemed calling which it had been to the previous generation. The social changes which came about after 1945 were many and various, and the railway authorities rapidly found they could no longer attract the large numbers of skilled, responsible men needed to keep the system moving. Railway operating conditions had irrevocably changed, and new methods and equipment were needed to ensure the survival of a railway network in the years ahead. Looking back from the later years of the 20th century it may be arguable that today's system is a satisfactory one, but for nearly three decades from 1950 the picture seemed progressively to darken as the years passed, almost to a point where railway services would be written off as socially unnecessary.

Back in 1946 the locomotive sheds of Leeds and Bradford held a collection of machinery of remarkable ancestry due, no doubt, to the needs of wartime operations. Copley Hill shed housed many 'V2' 2-6-2s and several ex-GCR locomotives, including the once-resplendent Atlantic type which, by this time, were no strangers to the West Riding. The stubby Ivatt 0-6-2 tank locomotives of Class 'N2' had had a long association with the Leeds and Bradford area until 1941 when 10 of the class were exchanged for a similar number of Class 'N1' locomotives. These were fully in evidence, and some still retained the condensing apparatus fitted for use in the London area. The carriage sidings here contained a mixture of stock originating from the former GER, GCR, NBR,

NER, GNR, M&GNJR, the Caledonian Railway (CR) and even the GWR. Within the carriage shed was the mothballed streamlined set which had been used on the 'West Riding Limited', the interiors shrouded with dust sheets and the carpets covered over. Gresley Pacifics were frequent visitors, of course, but the Peppercorn locomotives which were to be associated with the shed for almost 15 years were still a little way into the future. Neville Hill depot had a collection of locomotives

Top:

Ex-GCR locos often reached Copley Hill. 'B7' 4-6-0 No 5036 was photographed on shed on 21 July 1935. *W. L. Good*

Below:

Peppercorn 'A1' No 60114 *W. P. Allen* at Copley Hill on 30 March 1958, with sister locomotive No 60130 *Kestrel* stabled alongside. *D. Butterfield*

Bottom right:

The entrance to Copley Hill shed, with 'B1' 4-6-0 No 61016 *Inyala* and 'A4' Pacific No 60008 *Dwight D. Eisenhower* present on 19 March 1963.
J. S. Whiteley

including 'V2s', 'Hunt' class 4-4-0s, some ex-HBR tank engines, Sentinel locomotives and railcars, and the usual ex-NER 'Q6' 0-8-0s and, from 1949, 'B16' 4-6-0s. Small shunting engines abounded, particularly the Class 'G5' 0-4-4T machines. The 'B16' allocation of 1949 came about as a result of most of the class being dispersed away from York, where they had all spent the war years, and 19 more followed in 1951. The 'G5s' worked some local passenger services to Ilkley and Castleford, often on very smart timings, and the depot's allocation was only rendered redundant by the arrival of diesel railcars in the 1950s. Holbeck shed, the large and grimy depot along Nineveh Road, had a similar collection of antique machinery including compound 4-4-0s, ex-MR 0-4-4Ts and 0-6-0Ts alongside a fleet of 'Black Fives' and 'Jubilee' 4-6-0s. The Bradford depots told a similar story, with Manningham and Bowling sheds reflecting life at Holbeck and Copley Hill respectively. Low Moor was perhaps unique, with a strong LYR flavour to the allocation there — the 2-4-2 radial tanks and the odd remaining 'Dreadnought' 4-6-0 still being present. This depot was adjacent to large carriage sidings and, as at Copley Hill, the stock here in the late 1940s was a very

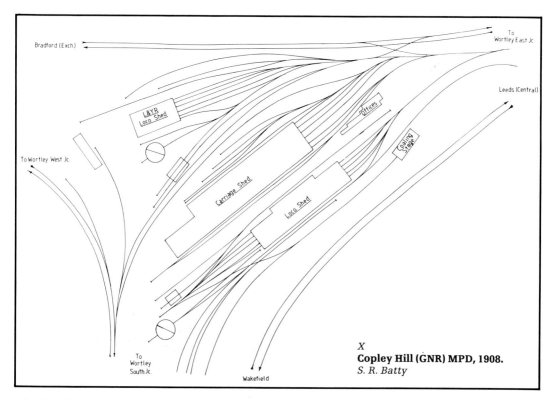

Bradford (Exch)

To
Wortley East Jc.

Leeds (Central)

L&YR
Loco Shed

Offices

To Wortley West Jc.

Coaling Stage

Carriage Shed

Loco Shed

To
Wortley
South Jc.

Wakefield

X
Copley Hill (GNR) MPD, 1908.
S. R. Batty

mixed collection indeed. The state of maintenance meant that almost any locomotive would
be pressed into service when required,
especially at peak periods or holiday times.
Records abound of passengers being hauled by
wheezing 'J6' 0-6-0 goods locomotives, ancient
GCR 4-6-0s and 4-4-2s and tiny ex-MR 0-4-4Ts.

Some Early Closures

Station closures did not commence until the
early 1950s, and the former GNR establish-

ments were particularly badly hit. Batley Carr
closed to passengers on 6 March 1950 and
Bowling Junction on 3 December 1951, and
Horton Park and St Dunstan's both closed on
15 September 1952. On the Bradford-Batley
line Dudley Hill closed from 7 April 1952,
Howden Clough from 1 December, Upper
Batley from 4 December and Birkenshaw &
Tong from 5 October 1953, leaving only
Laisterdyke and Drighlington & Adwalton
stations remaining open to passengers. Bees-

ton station, between Leeds and Ardsley, was closed on 2 March 1953, but the remaining stations to Wakefield survived into the 1960s. Another early closure took place at Dewsbury, where the remains of the MR's attempt to reach Bradford were further obliterated with the closure of Savile Town goods depot on 18 December 1950. Ravensthorpe (Lower), on the LYR spur from Heckmondwike to Thornhill, was closed on 30 June 1952 and Farnley & Wortley, on the ex-LNWR to Manchester, closed on 3 November 1952. (Churwell station had been built about halfway between Farnley and Morley, but was closed as a wartime measure from 2 December 1940. A similar fate had already overtaken Woodkirk, between Batley and Tingley, on 25 September 1939.)

Up to this point the closure appeared to have been somewhat piecemeal or random, but the first wholesale closure of a route to local passenger services took place on 5 October 1953, when all such services were withdrawn from the Leeds-Huddersfield 'New Line' stations. Parcels and freight traffic survived, and many expresses continued to use the route until final closure in 1964, but local passengers had to use the ex-LYR stations to reach Bradford, Mirfield or Wakefield. Whereas the 'New Line' survived for some years after losing its local passengers, the Queensbury lines lost all regular passenger services at one fell swoop on 23 May 1955. Closure occurred only after a public outcry; outrage which was heightened by the test running of new DMUs

over the routes, and by the continuing operation of freight trains. The final part of the route — the City Road goods depot — closed in 1972. The approaches to Keighley had been simplified and the signalboxes at Queensbury had been reduced to just one — the east box — by 1950, but the service had never made money and had incurred some awesome operating problems. A reverse curve in Lees Moor Tunnel combined with a stiff gradient to stop many a train within the confines of the wet and suffocating bore, and icicles hanging from the roof of Queensbury tunnel had often caused damage to locomotives. The number of passengers using the service was negligible, and complete closure to passengers was a foregone conclusion. In complete contrast to this was the Leeds-Stanningley-Bradford service, which was still buoyant and judged to be worthy of future investment. During 1951 an ex-GER 'N7' class 0-6-2T was used on the Leeds (Central)-Bradford (Exchange) service and gave rise to speculation that a service of auto-trains was to be introduced. Connecting traffic from Halifax and Bradford to King's Cross was still healthy, and was destined for an existence which was to be independent of the local services for many years ahead from 1951. Halifax portions were diverted away from the Queensbury route from 1952, giving a faster run directly via Low Moor, and the carriages for Wakefield usually went via Morley and were allowed only 27min for the none-too-easy 18-mile run. Class 'B1' 4-6-0 locomotives normally took these trains, but 'N1' 0-6-2Ts or LMS 2-6-4Ts would work to Halifax. The fast connections to Leeds of trains such as the 'Yorkshire Pullman' required some smart work indeed if the 17min schedule was to be kept, and again the 'N1s' were masters of this particular task.

Below:
Ardsley shed on 6 March 1960, with Hunslet shunter No D2591 and 'J52' 0-6-0ST No 68869 under repair. *D. Butterfield*

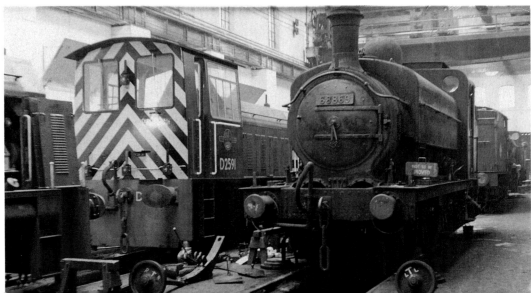

Arrival of the Multiple-Units

During September 1952 a former GWR diesel railcar was put to use in the Doncaster/ Wakefield area, perhaps as a brief trial for the possibilities of this form of traction in the West Riding. In December the British Transport Commission (BTC) announced a £500,000 'experiment' on DMU trains to be carried out in the area, which, it was claimed, had all the essential ingredients for giving the best return with the new trains. They were seen as an ideal weapon with which to fight road competition, and the West Riding had a large population in big industrial centres where the railway services would be greatly improved. The BTC hoped that the new diesel trains would be successful in applications across the country, but the Leeds and Bradford area was to be the testing-ground. Initial thoughts were to use the new trains initially in West Cumberland, with an installed engine output of 300hp provided by two 150hp engines, but the decision was then made to implement the West Riding scheme instead and employ 500hp

units. The two-car units were to be fitted with underfloor engines driving through a fluid flywheel and a preselector gearbox with freewheel facility, and were to be governed to a maximum speed of only 62mph. Body and underframe were made as one unit and the extensive use of light alloys ensured that one two-car unit weighed only 54 tons including fuel. This light weight and their place of origin — BR's Derby Works — gave the units the familiar name of 'Derby Lightweights'.

Up to four units could be coupled and driven together by one driver, and each unit could accommodate 114 third-class and 16 first-class passengers, with toilet facilities and space for parcels in the guard's compartment.

Top:
Ex-NER 'B15' 4-6-0 No 813 at Neville Hill, 21 July 1935. *W. L. Good*

Below:
Sentinel 'Y3' No 193 reposes inside Neville Hill, 21 July 1935. *W. L. Good*

Nameplate of 'D49/2' *The Staintondale*.
W. L. Good

Servicing was allocated to Bowling shed (more commonly known as Hammerton Street in BR days), which became the first depot in the country to receive the new trains. Services started on 14 June 1954 when a half-hourly service was introduced between Leeds (Central) and Bradford (Exchange), giving trains from Leeds between the hours of 08.06 and 23.06 and from Bradford between 05.35 and

Closure notice at Ovenden, 14 May 1955.
J. F. Oxley

22.35. Most trains ran via Stanningley, with some going via the Pudsey loop, and a few were reversed at Leeds to go on to Harrogate — on Sundays these were extended to the popular town of Knaresborough. The Derby Lightweight units were expected to replace over 309,000 miles of steam working per annum and give a total annual mileage of 520,000 and to attract £22,000 of extra business for a reduction in costs of £8,000 per annum. Apart from some alterations at Hammerton Street, very little (if any) civil engineering work appears to have been done. Leeds (Central) was closed for a short time in early May 1954 to allow renewal of some trackwork and Leeds 'B' signalbox, but this does not appear to have had any connection with the introduction of the DMUs. Another interesting, but unrelated, event noted at the same time was the laying-in of a connection to allow running into Central station from the ex-LNWR line at Farnley; this was, of course, the original route of 1848 and was still in place (though hardly used) by 1908. It is not certain when the connection was removed nor why it was replaced in 1954. Thoughts were certainly turning towards a complete rebuilding of the Leeds station layout by this time, and perhaps this was done as part of the first plans for coping with the construction work.

The DMUs got off to a very good start and fulfilled all expectations for the Leeds-Bradford service. Naturally there were a few hiccups, and steam power had to cover a failure on occasion. Harrogate trains seemed to suffer most, and 'N1' No 69445 was attached to five coaches and despatched from Leeds in fine style on 3 August 1954 to cover one such failure. Steam power was also prone to failure; on one occasion during the following month the Harrogate portion of an express from King's Cross was valiantly headed by a veteran 'G5' 0-4-4T, proudly bearing 'Class A' headlamps. Deliveries of the DMUs were slower than desired, and the North Eastern Region Modernisation Plan of 1956 stated that more

Facing page:
'J39' 0-6-0 No 64886 at Hammerton Street coaling plant on 8 January 1958, three days before the allocation was transferred to Low Moor.
G. W. Morrison

Inset:
Aspinall 0-6-0 No 52461 parked at Low Moor on 30 March 1958. Ex-LNER locos are visible in this scene, transferred from Hammerton Street earlier in the year. D. Butterfield

131

were required for the Leeds/Bradford service as well as to replace steam on the Ilkley and Skipton local trains. DMUs were introduced on the Leeds (Central)-Castleford (Central) and the Bradford (Exchange)-Wakefield (Westgate) via the Spen Valley services from 25 February 1957, but services for Keighley, Skipton, Ilkley and Leeds-Hull/Scarborough were a long way off. The Leeds/Bradford service was so successful that extra DMUs were still being called for by 1959, when takings were five times those of the final year of steam haulage and passenger figures were still climbing. This was a remarkable achievement in the face of strong road competition and, whereas the GNR/LNER efforts had achieved relatively little over almost 50 years, the BR plan succeeded almost overnight in comparison. Some other local features of the Plan covered the development of DMU facilities at Neville Hill depot, the rationalisation and improvement of goods depots, a new waiting room at Forster Square station and, last but not least, better loudspeakers at Leeds (City)!

During March 1958 more local services were dieselised. Most of the Leeds-Castleford and Bradford-Wakefield services had been extended to Pontefract and some from Bradford worked to Goole. One train daily worked from Bradford to Hull and another from Wakefield to Hull as from 3 March, and a new Leeds-Normanton-Wakefield-Barnsley service of 15 trains daily was introduced which gave good connections at Wakefield Kirkgate into the Goole trains. The new Barnsley service was successful, improving receipts by almost £15,000 in five months compared with the corresponding period of the previous year. During 1959 some first thoughts on improving the trans-Pennine services were made known, with plans being made for spending £1 million on a fleet of six-car, 1,840hp DMUs for the Hull-Liverpool run which would form part of a new regular interval service and would run from Leeds to Manchester in 1hr including stops at Huddersfield and Stalybridge. The Calder Valley would have a new DMU fleet to operate from Leeds (Central) to Manchester via Bradford (Exchange) and Halifax, again at regular intervals and with much faster journey times. These later DMUs were built as

Left:
'Jubilee' 4-6-0 No 45675 (formerly *Hardy*) leaves Forster Square with the 15.17 Heysham parcels on a sunny afternoon in October 1966. *J. S. Whiteley*

Below:
Class '5' 4-6-0 No 45373 accelerates a Leeds-Carlisle relief past the disused Armley Canal No 1 box on Good Friday 1967. *L. A. Nixon*

Above:
LMS '2P' 4-4-0 No 568 stands at Holbeck MPD on 26 August 1934. *W. L. Good*

Below:
The Midland 'Compound' 4-4-0 locomotives were no strangers to the Leeds area. LMS-built No 1086 is seen at Holbeck on 26 August 1934. *W. L. Good*

three-car units driven by four Rolls-Royce engines producing a total of 720hp, and went into service in 1962 with a regular departure time from Leeds (Central) of 6min past the hour. The Swindon-built 'Trans-Pennine' DMUs went into service during the summer of 1960 before the Newcastle-Liverpool route went over to 'Type 4' locomotive haulage, and passenger figures improved by 30% from Hull and Huddersfield and by no less than 45% from Leeds during the early weeks of operation. By mid-1961 the Newcastle service was fully dieselised and the regular interval service between Leeds and Liverpool was complete. Five 'Trans-Pennines' ran between Hull and Liverpool and return each day, four trains ran each way from Newcastle and Liverpool, and an hourly service from Leeds to Liverpool — half-hourly to and from Huddersfield — was the result.

Dieselisation

Main line diesel working commenced in early 1960, when an occasional English Electric Type 4 (late Class 40) locomotive reached Leeds from Newcastle in between workings on the East Coast main line. A batch of 13 locos was then sent to Gateshead depot for taking over the Liverpool turns during the spring of

1961, and by summer steam had been displaced from these jobs. Steam was still in charge of other turns to Newcastle from Leeds, however; Neville Hill still used Class 'A3' Pacifics on the 'Queen of Scots' via Harrogate and the 'North Briton' via York, but these were dieselised later in the summer. 'Peak' class locos were sent to Neville Hill at this time for Holbeck workings over the Midland main line, and the depot serviced these locomotives (Nos D11-D18) until Holbeck's diesel facilities were completed in late 1962. During 1960 this depot received an allocation of displaced Class 'A3' Pacifics, Nos 60038 *Firdaussi* and 60077 *The White Knight* arriving in the spring and Nos 60080 *Dick Turpin*, 60082 *Neil Gow*, 60088 *Book Law* and 60092 *Fairway* following in the summer. These locomotives were at first used on some Neville Hill freight duties before

Above:
The LMS 'Crab' 2-6-0s owed much of their appearance to a strong LYR influence in their design. No 2771 stands at Holbeck on 26 August 1934. *W. L. Good*

Below:
Holbeck 'Jubilee' No 45639 *Raleigh* stands on shed on 30 March 1958. *D. Butterfield*

being put to very good use on the Settle & Carlisle line, where their power output was a welcome improvement over the performances of 'Jubilee', 'Britannia' and 'Clan' class locos. The 'A3s' were actually cleared to work to Birmingham and Bristol, and even to work excursion traffic to Blackpool via Todmorden and Bury, but their final performances were played on the Carlisle road.

Above:

The remains of Johnson '1F' 0-6-0T No 41708, later preserved, dominate the scene at Holbeck on 18 March 1967, with Nos 44853 and D6786 in the background. *G. W. Morrison*

Copley Hill shed was still working the principal King's Cross expresses with steam power well into 1961. Immaculately-groomed Class 'A1' and 'A3' locomotives were a feature of this depot up to its closure in September 1964, when the duties were transferred to Holbeck. In early 1961 the shed's Class 'A1' and 'A3' locos shared a diagram which involved running to King's Cross and returning barely 1hr after arrival, giving a mileage of 372 per day. Easy enough for a new diesel, but good going indeed for 30-year-old steam locomotives. 'Deltic' diesels arrived in Leeds during 1961, when No D9003 ran a demonstration turn from King's Cross on 18 July to test the proposed winter timetable schedules for 1961/62. By the end that year Finsbury Park's 'Deltics' were giving some amazing performances on the 'West Riding' and 'Yorkshire Pullman' workings. Equally outstanding were some of the performances turned in by the Class 'A1', 'A3' and 'A4' Pacifics which were often called upon to cover a diesel failure — the trains had been increased considerably in weight but the

Pacifics generally made a good attempt at keeping time with the heavier, faster trains. The harsh winter of 1962 saw many problems with the new fleet, and once again the Pacifics saved the day. Dieselisation progressed during 1962 and steam working gradually declined, but even by early 1963 rostered steam jobs survived from Leeds Central. The up 'White Rose' was booked for Class 'A3' or 'A4' haulage right to the end of steam operation from King's Cross, and on 30 March No 60022 *Mallard* worked a round trip from Leeds, returning 5min early with the 400-ton down train. Steam into King's Cross officially finished on 15 June and the last booked arrival was Class 'A4' No 60025 *Falcon* with the up 'White Rose', but

this was followed later in the evening by No 60008 *Dwight D. Eisenhower* covering for a diesel failure. During this period the first Brush Type 4 locomotives (later Class 47) appeared in Leeds and were initially based at Neville Hill for crew training duties and, to cover a shortage of steam power at Copley Hill during the summer of 1963, two were borrowed during May for working between Bradford, Leeds and Doncaster. Nos D1502 and D1515 worked several Bradford portions of London expresses, and No D1502 first arrived in Exchange station on 1 June 1963 at the head of the 16.05 from King's Cross. Holbeck shed was modified during 1962-63 to provide diesel servicing facilities for an eventual fleet of

about 120 locomotives. The old machine shop was adapted for diesel repairs and a new dead-ended building was also erected. By the end of 1961 more of the depot's steam allocation had been dispersed, and four 'Royal Scot' 4-6-0s, Nos 46109 *Royal Engineer*, 46113 *Cameronian*, 46117 *Welsh Guardsman* and 46130 *The West Yorkshire Regiment* were displaced from the Settle & Carlisle line by diesel power and transferred to Low Moor shed, where their use was somewhat restricted as they were not allowed to work to Leeds or Liverpool on the principal Low Moor duties. The 'Scots' were quickly placed in store, and were withdrawn during early 1963 when new 'Type 2' and 'Type 3' diesels were allocated to Leeds. Some of the 'Scots' were stored at Farnley Junction and, occasionally, it was possible to see these locomotives in the company of one of the Holbeck Class 'A3s' sent to Farnley for light repairs or washing-out during the time when construction work on the diesel depot made these activities impossible.

Developments at Bradford during the early 1960s were rather few, perhaps the biggest change being the complete changeover made at Hammerton Street from steam to multiple-unit working during 1961. A total of 85 railcars were maintained there at the time with a further 60 expected in the near future. Also based at the depot were 19 shunters which had taken over many of the duties previously carried out by steam locomotives at Adolphus Street, City Road, Laisterdyke, Stanningley and Pudsey. The depot needed very little alteration, and plants for fuelling and washing were quickly installed. Three roads of the 11 in the shed building were parted off and used for a heavy maintenance shop, and the old lifting shop was used for similar work on the new allocation. On the ex-MR side of the city, the KWVR branch was dieselised during the summer of 1960 using DMUs based at Manningham shed which usually stabled overnight at Keighley. Bradford's goods depots were greatly reduced during this period; Vicar Lane had closed in April 1958 and Bridge Street closed from 22 October 1962, whilst Trafalgar Street and Valley Road combined together from this date. Adolphus Street and City Road continued in use until May 1972, although City Road received only coal deliveries from June 1967 onwards.

Three serious runaways occurred at Bradford during the 1960s, unfortunately with some loss of life. In January 1963 Low Moor Class '5' No 44695 ran away with the 06.15 Low Moor-Springmill Street goods and came to rest within 12ft of a 40ft drop into Bridge Street Goods Depot and, on 3 June 1964, the same locomotive, while standing in Platform 4 at Exchange station, was hit by a runaway DMU forming the 16.25 Manchester Victoria-Leeds. This resulted in the death of the DMU driver and two passengers. On 10 November 2-6-0 No 43072 with a train of 21 empty wagons from Ardsley ran away from Laisterdyke and entered Adolphus Street at almost 50mph, the locomotive crashing through some buffer stops and falling into the street below. Miraculously, no one was hurt. The loco was cut up and removed by a local scrap merchant.

Below:
Amazingly, the former steam shed at Bowling survived almost intact after the allocation was transferred away to make room for Hammerton Street's DMU fleet. This July 1987 view shows the scene at the now-closed diesel depot. *S. R. Batty*

Modernisation

Several more stations closed during this period, with Marsh Lane (on the realigned 1869 entry to Leeds [New]) closing on 15 September 1958 and the infamous Holbeck stations going on 7 July of the same year. Osmondthorpe Halt closed on 7 March 1960 and both Hunslet and Lofthouse & Outwood went on 13 June. More ex-GNR stations were closed too, such as Morley on 2 January 1961, Drighlington & Adwalton on 1 January 1962, both Batley and Dewsbury (Central) on 7 September 1964 and Ardsley on 2 November. One particularly bad loss was the Pudsey loop, where both stations were closed from 15 June 1964 and compensation was made by the usual bus service plus an extra two trains being provided at Stanningley! Closure proceedings were also

Above:
Low Moor interior on 24 September 1967, just one week before the end. *G. W. Morrison*

Below:
2-6-4T locomotives Nos 42116 and 42055 and 'B1' 4-6-0 No 61388 inside Low Moor shed on 19 March 1966. *D. Butterfield*

initiated for three more lengths of railway during 1964 which were to see some significant changes made to the railway services during the following year. The three lines affected were the ex-L&BR route from Leeds to Bradford via Shipley, the ex-LYR Spen Valley route from Low Moor to Mirfield and Thornhill, and the Leeds 'New Line' from Heaton Lodge to Farnley Junction. The Shipley route was to lose the local stopping trains but would still be open for expresses to Carlisle and Scotland and for the Lancaster/Morecambe traffic, whilst the other two lost all passenger services. Freight operation on the Spen Valley line continued until 1981 and the route was later acquired by the West Yorkshire Transport Museum for conversion into an inter-urban tramway. The Bradford-Wakefield (Westgate) service was still quite well-used and also generated a reasonable parcels traffic, but the annual loss was still claimed to be almost £40,000. Local traffic had disappeared from the 'New Line' in 1953 and the goods traffic had been whittled away between 1960 and 1963, leaving only a few express workings and several tanker trains to the Charrington-Hargreaves fuel depot at Liversedge as the only users of the line. The closure of the ex-L&BR route was allowed and

the Leeds-Shipley-Bradford locals ceased from 22 March 1965 and Low Moor and the Spen Valley stations at Heckmondwike, Liversedge and Cleckheaton closed from 14 June. A rather more protracted string of events led to the 'New Line' closure, starting with plans being made for a new connection from the Thornhill-Heckmondwike (LYR) line to Heckmondwike (Goods) on the LNWR line to allow oil trains to continue running to Liversedge after closure of the remainder of the line, an operation which ceased during the mid-1980s. Three or four trains ran weekly in each direction to and from Ellesmere Port, and this was exactly the sort of traffic which BR wanted. The line's goods depots closed in late August 1964 and all the expresses bar one — the 15.00 Liverpool-Newcastle — were to be diverted away by 7 September. This last train was to be re-routed via Dewsbury from December, but four objections were received and the closure date of 7 January 1965 had to be postponed. This was just as well, because continuing permanent way and civil engineering work at Dewsbury saw the 'New Line' being used for diversions throughout the early months of 1965. The closure was then formally allowed despite the objections and yet another date — 14 June — was set for final closure. Once

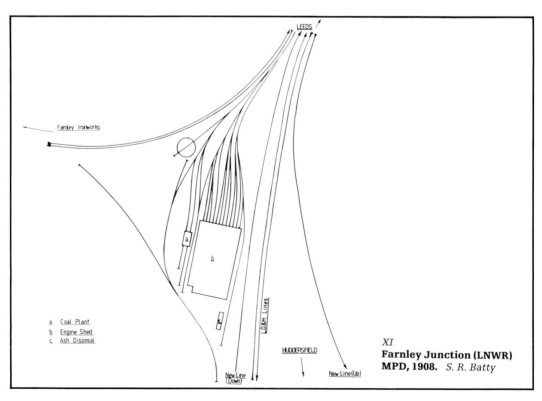

XI
Farnley Junction (LNWR) MPD, 1908. *S. R. Batty*

again, the work at Dewsbury ensured another postponement and the last train actually ran on 31 July 1965, when Class 40 No D395 hauled the 15.00 from Liverpool over the line for the last time. The new Heckmondwike connection was duly laid in and the oil depot was then served by a joint LYR/LNWR access from Thornhill Junction from 11 January 1966.

The elimination of the Leeds-Shipley-Bradford passenger service was an integral part of the modernisation plan for the new Leeds (City) station, where all Bradford services were to be concentrated on the Stanningley line via a new station at Dawson's Corner and a new alignment to give access into City station from Whitehall Junction. Two other fundamental changes to local routes involved traffic for Huddersfield and for King's Cross — the former was to be concentrated on the original LD&MR approach through Copley Hill and down to Whitehall Junction, and the latter was to use the former 'Viaduct Route' to a new junction with the ex-GNR line at Gelderd

Junction. Thus, trains for King's Cross would actually have a choice of two routes to Gelderd Junction (the original Copley Hill line was retained with suitable alterations at the approach to Whitehall) and the western end of the 1882 'Viaduct Route' from Farnley Junction was abandoned. The idea of having a single main line station in Leeds went back to the hectic days of the 1850s but circumstances conspired to delay the project into the 1950s before any real progress was made. During 1958 City station handled 2¾ million passengers and Central dealt with no less than 2¼ million, as well as a vast amount of parcels traffic generated between the two. A plan for a £4½ million station was put to the BTC in 1959 for completion by 1963, when full dieselisation would allow the most benefit to be reaped from the proposals. Two more through platforms were to be created and some platforms would be lengthened, but the total platform length was to be reduced from 14,000ft to 12,600ft and water for locomotives was to be provided

Above:
Class 37 Co-Co No D6878 crosses over to the fast line at Heaton Lodge on 8 September 1967. The partly-dismantled 'New Line' is in the background, and Battyeford viaduct is clearly visible behind the left-hand signal gantry. *B. J. Ashworth*

Left:
The remains of Cleckheaton LNWR station in October 1987. *S. R. Batty*

Right:

A small section of the 'New Line' remains today at Liversedge. The siding on the right leads into the oil terminal, and the single track leads to Heckmondwike. Although intact in September 1987, no traffic has used the branch for some time and its future is uncertain.
S. R. Batty

Below right:

Another view of No 45675 *Hardy*, this time at Whitehall Junction with the 09.33 Morecambe-Leeds (City) on 16 June 1962. *D. I. Wood*

Below:

The area outside Leeds (City) was greatly remodelled during the rebuilding of the station. 2-6-0 No 43043 leaves the station with a lengthy parcels train and passes Canal Junction, with the viaduct lines leaving off to the right. *G. T. Robinson*

throughout the station — electric train heating was still far from universal on BR! Two interesting proposals were made which never materialised in the completed scheme due to a cutback on expenditure ordered in 1961; these were plans for the King's Cross traffic to be run on a flyover above the Whitehall area, and also for a car park to be built in the new station which could be extended both upwards, on successive decks, and downwards into the 'Dark Arches' below the platforms.

Plans had been produced for such a station in 1948, but shortage of cash kept these on the shelf until 1959. After the 1961 cutback a rather cheaper scheme was drawn up, but this included a resignalling programme and re-alignment to all exits from the west of the station except those to Normanton and Skipton. The latter route did not escape completely unscathed, as the withdrawal of the local passenger service was followed by removal of the fast lines from Armley (Canal) to Kirkstall and from Apperley to Thackley, including the southern bore of Thackley tunnel. Work started during November 1959 with the renewal of the canal bridge, in an area where a great deal of work was ultimately done in order to level up the tracks and give the necessary freedom for the new layout. The new push-button signalling system initially only covered 18 route miles but replaced 17 mechanical boxes, and it was to be greatly extended over the following years — one plan was for the entire 'Viaduct Route' and the new Gelderd Junction eventually to be abandoned when the new system could cope with sending all such traffic via Whitehall and the new Holbeck junctions, but this was not to materialise for over 20 years. Work progressed slowly and it was not until May 1966 that the main structural work was completed. Platforms 1 to 6 in the Wellington area were largely filled-in and extended for use as a parcels depot and car park, and the new roof at the New station end was built to give sufficient clearance for 25kV overhead wiring, which it was felt would, one day, reach the city. Some further work remained to be done when Central station finally closed on 29 April 1967, after more than 110 years of grimy, pungent toil in the service of so many railway users.

Steam's Grand Finale

The end of steam traction based in Leeds and Bradford came in the autumn of 1967, but the last couple of years leading to the fateful event were packed with interest for devotees of steam from far and wide. Steam declined slowly throughout the 1960s but many duties remained steam-hauled until late 1967, including several front-rank passenger workings. During 1965 and early 1966 there was a shortage of diesel power for the Leeds-Huddersfield-Manchester service which regularly saw 'Britannia' Pacifics in use on the Liverpool and Newcastle expresses either as rostered or substitute power. These locomotives were based in the Manchester area — usually Stockport — and were regular visitors to Farnley Junction shed at this time.

Other workings, such as the daily Newcastle-Manchester (Red Bank) newspaper empties, the 15.20 Wavertree goods, the 20.15 Stockport vans, the 22.06 Manchester parcels and the 22.42 South Wales mail, all provided regular employment for Farnley's collection of LMSR Class '5s', BR Standard '9Fs', 'Britannias' and the occasional 'Jubilee' or 'Crab'. Heavy oil trains from Ellesmere Port were worked in by Class '9F' 2-10-0s or '8F' 2-8-0s, usually double-headed, and several daily trip workings were made by assorted 2-6-0s and 4-6-0s to Healey Mills. A regular daily working was run from Copley Hill sidings to a local steel stockholder's yard and was the preserve of Farnley's 'Jinty' 0-6-0 tank locos. These small engines regularly hauled heavy trains along the branch past the shed without any difficulty, despite facing a stiff climb away from the main line. Just occasionally a visiting engine would be put to work on the branch, and it was then that trouble always seemed to happen — clear memories exist of an ex-LNWR 0-8-0 wheezing and panting around the curve at an ever-falling rate of progression before expiring alongside the spur to the coaling plant! The 'Jinties' were the masters of many jobs until their replacement during 1964 by BR Standard 2-6-0s, which also took over the shunting at the ex-LNWR goods depot below Central station. Even these did not survive long before replacement by Class 08 shunters, and by early 1966 the writing was clearly on the wall for Farnley Junction shed. More diesel power was arriving and Farnley men used Neville Hill locos for a brief period during February before full dieselisation of the Leeds trans-Pennine workings followed in the summer. The allocation was gradually whittled away by withdrawals or dispersal to Holbeck, Low Moor, Wakefield or Mirfield and closure took place in November 1966, with complete demolition following during October 1967. The original LNWR Leeds shed was located in the area around Gelderd and Wortley Junctions, but this was demolished and the materials recovered for use in the new

Above:

Class 46 No 46026 *Leicestershire and Derbyshire Yeomanry,* **the only member of its class to be named, awaits departure with a Manchester train on 28 August 1979.** *J. E. Oxley*

Right:

Holbeck MPD, 28 August 1967. *J. S. Whiteley*

Top right:

Class '3F' 0-6-0 No 43586 and Class '2' 2-6-2T No 41273 at Manningham shed on 2 August 1961. *D. Butterfield*

Farnley shed which was opened in 1885. Farnley Junction signalbox closed from 18 December 1966, when all traffic was diverted away from the 'Viaduct Route' and on to the Copley Hill-Whitehall Junction line. Despite the full dieselisation of the Manchester services, steam power was still used occasionally right up to the end of 1967, when locos still based in Manchester were called upon to cover a diesel failure and work into Leeds where no servicing facilities existed and even getting a refill of water could be a problem.

Steam working out of Leeds and Bradford towards Lancaster and Carlisle was very much in evidence during 1966, with 'Black Fives', 'Jubilees', 'Britannias', 'Clans' and '9Fs' regularly working to Carlisle and assorted 4-6-0 classes reaching Lancaster from Leeds and Bradford until the DMUs took over in April. By early 1967 five 'Jubilees' were based at Holbeck in readiness for one final, glorious summer fling which was to mark the end of their association with the Settle & Carlisle in no uncertain manner. Nos 45562 *Alberta*, 45593 *Kolhapur*, 45647 *Sturdee*, 45675 *Hardy* and 45697 *Achilles* were the locos involved to a greater or lesser extent — Nos 45562 and 45593 took the lion's share, with Nos 45675 and 45697 suffering earlier withdrawal. Easter saw the relief 'Thames-Clyde Express' in the hands of No 45647 and 'Britannias' Nos 70048 and 70053, but the Saturday 10.17 Leeds-Glasgow became a star turn which was 'Jubilee'-worked throughout the summer timetable, along with a morning St Pancras-Glasgow relief which changed locos at Whitehall Junction at 14.15 before continuing northwards. Holbeck shed lost its steam allocation from 2 October 1967, and the 'Long Drag' ceased to echo to the full-blooded, three-cylinder roar of a 'Jubilee' at full charge towards Ais Gill summit.

Services from Bradford to Wakefield continued to enjoy steam haulage until autumn 1967, using the direct route via the Wortley curve. The locomotives were provided by Low Moor shed and any attention required was given either at the parent depot or at Wakefield. Copley Hill shed was closed from 9 September 1964 when the duties were transferred to Holbeck and the surviving locos to Neville Hill or Ardsley. Most of the Class 'A1' Pacifics survived another year until four were withdrawn from Neville Hill during late 1965, but the last survivors hung on until March 1965 with a few jobs from York shed.

Steam on the ex-GNR line was quickly eliminated and the sheds were equally quickly demolished — Copley Hill was razed in October 1965, by which time Ardsley was also closed and on the way to oblivion. The Morley route between Bradford and Wakefield was earmarked for total closure, and by mid-1965 only the 15.08 portion for King's Cross was being routed this way — the line from Adwalton Junction to Batley (East) was already being lifted. By July 1966 this last train was diverted via Wortley, although the Morley line had seen extra use by diverted trains during the building of New Pudsey station from September 1966. Sulzer Type 2 diesels were expected to displace the Low Moor 2-6-4 tank locos at one period in 1966, but this did not happen and the ex-LMSR fleet continued in service until the end of the 1967 summer. The King's Cross portions serving Bradford were usually of three coaches only,

Right:
'Britannia' No 70034, formerly *Thomas Hardy,* **stands at Manningham on 21 March. The loco has probably worked into Bradford with a train from Carlisle.**
G. W. Morrison

Below right:
A Skipton local gets away from Forster Square behind 2-6-0 No 46442 in March 1956. *P. Ransome-Wallis*

Far right, top:
Manningham Junction signalbox on 17 August 1951. *D. Butterfield*

Far right, bottom:
The last days of steam power at Neville Hill. Class 'A1' 4-6-2 No 60154 *Bon Accord* **and 'Q6' 0-8-0 No 63426 are seen inside the depot on 9 February 1964.** *G. W. Morrison*

and many enthusiastic crews — particularly those with a young fireman — rattled these trains through Beeston at 75mph on the climb to Ardsley tunnel. Low Moor was a busy shed even at this late stage, and summer Saturdays saw the depot sending locos to Blackpool, Sheffield and Manchester as well as to Wakefield. Several 'B1' class 4-6-0s ended their days here, and No 61306 ran two return trips to Leeds on 30 September 1967, the last official day of steam haulage between Leeds and Bradford. 'Jubilees' were also used, and No 45565 *Victoria* worked the 08.55 Leeds (Central)-Blackpool regularly during the summer of 1965, using the Laisterdyke-Bowling Junction line to avoid reversal at

Exchange station. A nightly Leeds-Halifax parcels also used this line, but both trains disappeared before Low Moor shed finally closed on 2 October 1967. The shed dated back to 1866, and alterations were made in 1890 and 1945 by the LYR and LMSR respectively. Passenger work had been the shed's principal diet for a stud of assorted locomotives including 'Radial Tanks', 'Dreadnoughts', 'Black Fives' and 'Jubilees', but several freight and mixed traffic locos appeared — classes 'J6', 'J39' and 'B1' — when Bowling's steam allocation was dispersed. *Victoria* was the shed's last 'Jubilee', but others of a longer-standing tenure included *Warspite, Repulse, Vindictive* and *Ulster.*

The surviving steam locomotives were shuffled around as sheds closed, and ended up being concentrated at Low Moor or Wakefield. Neville Hill closed to steam power during June 1966 and three ex-NER 'Q6' 0-8-0s went to Normanton and one even to Farnley Junction, and a pair of 2-6-4 tanks were sent to Low Moor. The 'Q6's had no regular work and were merely stored pending withdrawal, whilst the 2-6-4s were actively employed from Bradford (Exchange). Wakefield MPD became the last home of a large fleet of ex-War Department 2-8-0s accumulated from far and wide, and the total allocation of this class reached almost 100 by the end of 1965 when Ardsley had closed. Mirfield was used briefly as a diesel stabling point, but this shed and Huddersfield both closed from 2 January 1967 when the Mirfield locos went to Wakefield and the Huddersfield allocation was sent to Normanton.

Bradford's Manningham shed closed in April 1967 and, once again, more 2-6-4 tank locos found their way to Low Moor. By early 1967

Above left:
A little later in the same year, 'Q6' No 63348 is parked alongside ex-Copley Hill 'A1' No 60134 *Foxhunter* on 10 May. *G. W. Morrison*

Left:
On the last day of steam working, 1 October 1967, 2-6-4T No 42152 awaits departure from Bradford (Exchange) with the 10.20 through coaches for King's Cross. *J. B. Mounsey*

Above:
The simultaneous departures of the Saturdays-only trains for Skegness and Bridlington at 08.20 became a regular attraction for enthusiasts during 1967. Class '5' 4-6-0s 44694 and 44662 pass Mill Lane with the two trains on 29 July of that year. *V. C. K. Allen*

over half of the freight workings along the Calder Valley were still steam-hauled, and Wakefield and Normanton depots had the job of patching and mending the incoming locos for return to their home depots across the Pennines. By the middle of the year, however, the Healey Mills 'Type 3' and 'Type 4' fleet had largely taken over this work and Wakefield shed closed from 3 June, leaving the depot to be used as a dumping ground for the fleets of locomotives destined for breaking up at Hull.

Steam motive power was still very active when the official end came in October 1967 and the allocations of Holbeck, Low Moor and Normanton were disbanded and largely put into store pending removal for scrap. The Low Moor 2-6-4 tanks and the last three Class 'B1' 4-6-0s (Nos 61030, 61306, 61337) were in use to the end, and on 1 October, Holbeck had nearly 30 locos on shed including 'Jubilee' 4-6-0s Nos 45562, 45593 and 45697 and 'Britannia' class 4-6-2s Nos 70004 and 70029. After this date the arriving locomotives from the Calder Valley line were serviced at Normanton, an arrangement which petered out with final dieselisation in early 1968. It was the end of an era, and the railways of Leeds and Bradford suddenly became rather antiseptic and soulless after years of providing interest and variety for generations of enthusiasts. But greater changes lay ahead.

149

7 Recent Developments

During late 1967 an inspection of the Bridge Street road bridge above the platform ends at Exchange station revealed some very severe corrosion damage which, it was estimated, would take almost two years to repair. As well as this the fabric of the station itself was in a very poor state and it was felt to be far too big for the traffic which was handled there by the end of the 1960s. Bradford Corporation wanted to build a new, central bus station in the city centre and the need for renewal of Exchange station provided the Corporation and BR with an opportunity to create a purpose-built transport interchange which would be a great boon to the city. Talks began in 1969 and centred around using the site of Bridge Street goods depot for a bus station and garage and building a two-island platform station to the south of the existing terminus. Many delays occurred and work did not start on the site until early 1972, some 12 months after the initial hoped-for completion date, and the last platforms at Exchange were taken out of use by the end of the year. Rail facilities at the new four-platform station came into use during the following summer, but the fully-integrated road/rail interchange was not completed until March 1978.

Whereas Exchange station was demolished and replaced by a clinically-modern structure of utterly forgettable appearance and utilitarian fitness for purpose, the sleeping giant of Forster Square station was allowed to be

Below:

Interchange station is a much humbler establishment than the now-demolished Exchange. Class 46 'Peak' No 46026 *Leicestershire and Derbyshire Yeomanry* departs with ecs for Neville Hill off the Weymouth-Bradford train on 14 August 1982. *L. A. Nixon*

downgraded to a two-platform shed serving only Skipton and Keighley from within its vast emptiness. Parcels traffic ebbed away and by late 1984 the station was serving only the local trains to these destinations, the nearby yards at Valley Road having disappeared also. Today, the station remains in this state of near-abandonment with the still-impressive frontage almost hidden from view and the local trains using a short length of each of two platforms, and the recently-diverted long distance trains using the long-disused platforms adjacent to the parcels area.

The creation of the West Yorkshire Passenger Transport Executive (WYPTE) in 1974 reversed the ever-falling totals of passengers using the local railway network once the PTE had got into its stride during the early 1980s. This long delay is explained by the terrible mess into which local passenger transport had fallen by the early 1970s, and the vast amount of work needed in order to establish a coherent policy which would integrate road and rail transport and get the travelling public back on to buses and trains. By 1972, when the Transport Act setting up the PTEs was passed, the West Yorkshire railway network was in rapid decline and many areas were either rail-less or served very poorly by almost non-existent services. The Leeds-Bradford 'Short line' was devoid of stations except for New Pudsey; Forster Square-Shipley was

stationless and many lines ran through urban areas where potential traffic existed but where the local station had been closed many years previously without any thought being given to future needs. The story of how WYPTE looked at the problems and created solutions using money from various sources is beyond the scope of this book, but the result has been the introduction of a new fleet of DMUs, a continual programme of station building in urban areas, and greatly-increased frequency of train services. In the immediate Leeds/Bradford area new stations have appeared or been reopened at Bramley, Crossflatts, Frizinghall, East Garforth, Altofts, Cottingley and Oulton (Baildon being reopened in 1972 by Bradford Corporation) and more stations being built towards the West Yorkshire boundaries. Some services have been rescued from what would have been certain closure, such as Leeds/Bradford-Ilkley and Wakefield-Huddersfield, and others were rescued before the rot had set in too far, such as Leeds/

Below:
Bradford's Forster Square station may be rejuvenated by the diversion of long-distance traffic for Interchange station. A Class 142 DMU stands at the shortened platform on 27 January 1988. *S. R. Batty*

Top:
A Class 144 DMU departs from Forster Square on 27 January 1988. *S. R. Batty*

Above:
Class 47 No 47526 *Northumbria*, **sporting nameplates once carried by now-withdrawn No 47405, accelerates through Wortley with the 08.42 Leeds-Carlisle on 5 August 1987.** *S. R. Batty*

Right:
Work has just started on the new Frizinghall station as Class 142 unit No 142083 passes with the 11.30 Guiseley train on 5 August 1987. *S. R. Batty*

Bradford-Skipton, and Leeds-Castleford-Goole.

Services from Leeds to Bradford and to Wakefield are now very good, with trains running approximately every 20min and on reasonably rapid schedules. The Wakefield service has benefited from new hourly 'Sprinter' trains to Sheffield running via Westgate station and Moorthorpe, and the Leeds-Wakefield (Kirkgate)-Barnsley trains have been diverted to reverse at Castleford, so giving this Aire Valley town much better links to Leeds and Wakefield.

Not all developments have been so positive, however. Rationalisation and closures have continued to affect the railway geography of Leeds and Bradford. The transfer of through trains from the former MR main line has led to partial closure of the route and the abolition of Goose Hill Junction — the point at which the MR and LYR lines converged.

In Bradford, the short freight links to Dudley Hill and to the English Electric Co had been closed by 1987. The Laisterdyke to Bowling Junction line, which had lost its passenger services in the late 1960s and which had been severed at the Laisterdyke end, was closed in 1986. Even the last motive power depot in Bradford, Hammerton Street, was closed, in 1985.

After some 15 years of high-speed haulage by the 'Deltics' the Leeds/Bradford-King's Cross services were taken over by the new HST fleet from May 1979 onwards, the 'Deltics' not finally disappearing from the ECML until 2 January 1982. Initially the fastest 'Deltic' average speed of 79mph was only raised to just over 81mph but, by 1984, the fastest average had been raised to almost 88mph due to track and signalling improvements and the virtual elimination of locomotive-hauled trains. Unfortunately, by 1983 Bradford's direct connections with King's Cross were very few indeed as most trains had been diverted away from the Wortley curve, adjacent to the site of Copley Hill MPD, to run into Leeds and reverse thence to King's Cross. The City of Bradford Metropolitan District Council and the local TUCC were extremely concerned at this negative development, and protests were made when the last remaining King's Cross train to use the curve, the up 'Bradford Executive', was diverted away from May 1984. The down train had been similarly re-routed a year previously, and from May 1985 the last train to use the curve — a weekend Castleford-Blackpool train — was diverted away. Shortly afterwards the junction at the south end of the curve was removed, thus rendering the line unusable for through traffic and cutting off Bradford's last independent access to King's Cross. Feelings in Bradford were also strengthened at this time when the decision was announced that although the ECML was to be electrified (after at least 30 years of talking about it) and the Leeds service was to be the first to be completed, there was no intention to carry the wires into Bradford. The city saw itself as condemned to relying on multiple-unit connections with Leeds and becoming more of a railway backwater than ever before, and legal action on behalf of the City and the TUCC quickly followed against BR on the basis that the Wortley line had been closed without the formalities of Section 56 of the 1962 Transport Act being followed. The High Court judgement proved to be in favour of the City of Bradford and the TUCC during April 1987, and was upheld by the Appeal Court later in the year when BR attempted to reverse the ruling. What happens next remains to be seen, and will depend on the interpretation of the judgements given and on the retrospective procedures of Section 56 as implemented by all parties who can claim evidence of hardship suffered should the line be taken out of use.

The electrification issue remains topical, to say the least, at the time of writing. Rapid progress resulted in the planned start of services to Leeds being brought forward from October 1989 to August 1988, when the occcasional use of electric haulage was to take place as and when availability permitted. Meanwhile, BR's hard attitude against extending the scheme to Bradford has softened very slightly with some radical alterations being made to InterCity services from Bradford during 1988. Long-distance trains were taken away from the Interchange station and diverted into Shipley and Forster Square on the assumption that a vast, untapped market existed in north Bradford for inter-city travel. Travellers from the south Bradford area, it was stated, had for many years been driving to Leeds or Wakefield and would continue to do so, not being tempted back to Interchange station. Thus Interchange will concentrate on the Leeds-Bradford-Halifax-Manchester service and Forster Square, after suffering 20 years of neglect, could well become the city's principal long-distance station if the two-year experiment yields satisfactory results by October 1990.

It is this outcome which may yet see the 25kV scheme extended to Bradford, for BR have stated that it is up to Bradford's railway users to demonstrate that such a scheme would be worthwhile. Money could well be

Above:
Winter sun warms the razed site of Low Moor MPD on 27 January 1988. *S. R. Batty*

found from alternative sources such as European Community grants (available because of the city's social needs and problems of unemployment), Bradford Council itself and the West Yorkshire Passenger Transport Authority (WYPTA). It would be ironic indeed if the wires were eventually erected over the long-underused ex-LBR route via Shipley, instead of the shorter route via New Pudsey which has carried all express traffic, albeit at constantly-decreasing levels, for over 20 years.

The PTA have long been considering the viability of a cross-Bradford link, initially as a cross-city light railway but more recently as a full-gauge connection between Interchange and Forster Square. The Calder Valley service from Manchester could be diverted through Shipley to Leeds, and the Skipton/Ilkley trains routed via Interchange and New Pudsey. This scheme is part of a long-term strategy for the area looking well into the next century, but the possibilities of such a scheme are interesting to say the least. The idea certainly will not go away — it has been around since the 1840s and

if it did finally happen then it would probably arrive about 100 years after the MR started their bold move at the end of the 19th century.

During October 1987 the Leeds Viaduct line was taken out of use and the Gelderd Junction of 1967 was removed, so realising a threat which was originally voiced at the time of the City station rebuilding during the 1960s. The line was left out of the electrification plans right from the start and many observers saw the writing on the wall from then. Both the measures adopted by the LNWR to give better access to Leeds have, therefore, now been eliminated, and another taste of irony came to the railway scene when doubts were expressed in early 1988 about the ability of the Whitehall Junction area to cope with the high local traffic flows expected later in the year! Despite problems with new rolling-stock which have kept too many worn out DMUs in service, and many arguments which have centred on the issue of paying for local services through the rates, the PTA services have almost been too successful! The local stations are well-used, the trains run almost on a bus-service frequency, and they are full of passengers. Railways in the Leeds and Bradford area have been packed with fascinating interest for over 150 years, and present trends indicate this will continue — both on local and main line services — well into the future.

Appendix 1
Allocation of Locomotives, 1933

Low Moor

MR Class '2P' 4-4-0: 678-680

MR Compound '4P' 4-4-0: 1185-1188

LYR '4P' 4-6-0: 5806/8/38/9/40/2

LNWR 0-8-0: 8962

LYR Class '2P' 4-4-2: 10309/10/20/2/35

LYR 'Dreadnought' 4-6-0: 10405/12/3/7/42

LYR Aspinall Class '2P' 2-4-2T: 10665, 10700/13/17/35/6/47/55/60/1/89/90, 10804/8/40/1/85/90, 10945/6

LYR 0-6-0ST: 11426, 11495

LYR 0-6-0T: 11512

LYR Class '2F'/'3F' 0-6-0: 12089, 12239/43/54/7, 12354, 12410/35/51, 12520/39/90

LYR 0-8-0: 12823/65, 12933

LMS 'Crab' 2-6-0: 13015/6/9/22/3, 13165

Manningham

MR 2-4-0: 204/19

MR Class '2P' 4-4-0: 479/83

MR Class '1P' 0-4-4T: 1251/5/63/75/7/90/3/5/6/8, 1300/53/4/6, 1407

MR Class '1F' 0-6-0T: 1678

MR Class '3F' 0-6-0: 1952/4/5, 2926, 3018/27/65, 3276/95, 3346/51, 3479, 3558, 3746/83/4, 16502/3

LYR Aspinall Class '2P' 2-4-2T: 10625-7/9-32/6/7

LYR Class '3F' 0-6-0: 12135/6

Bowling

Robinson Class 'B6' 4-6-0: 5053, 5416

Ivatt Class 'C12' 4-4-2T: 4009A, 4013/7/8/20, 4528/30/6/9

Stirling Class 'J1' 0-6-0: 3004-6/8/9

Stirling Class 'J2' 0-6-0: 3071/80

Stirling Class 'J3' 0-6-0: 3398, 4086/8/93, 4105/18/34/46/7/52/3/7

Stirling Class 'J4' 0-6-0: 3304, 4090

Gresley Class 'J50' 0-6-0T: 583/8/9/91, 1037/45, 3159/62/4/6/70/4, 3223/33/4

Ivatt Class 'J52' 0-6-0ST: 3930/67, 4053, 4215/72

Stirling Class 'J54' 0-6-0ST: 3908

Stirling Class 'J55' 0-6-0ST: 3859

Ivatt Class 'N1' 0-6-2T: 4564/8/9/72/4/93/4

Gresley Class 'N2' 0-6-2T: 2583/4/7/90, 2688

Robinson Class 'Q4' 0-8-0: 5135, 6178

Holbeck — including locomotives sub-shedded at Stourton

MR Class '2P' 4-4-0: 342/65, 480/2/4, 546/7

LMS Class '2P' 4-4-0: 565/9

LMS Compound '4P' 4-4-0: 1009-13/70/1/85-8

MR Class '1P' 0-4-4T: 1279, 1329, 1405/16

MR Class '1F' 0-6-0T: 1686/92, 1745/8/66, 1842/59

MR Class '3F' 0-6-0: 2921-3/5/7/9/61/75, 3138, 3307/50, 3429/46/8/9/51/6/7/68/9/76/84, 3579, 3610/30/46, 3714/31/9/42/4/53

MR Class '4F' 0-6-0: 3851-5, 3929/87/93-8

LMS Class '4F' 0-6-0: 4095, 4128, 4238/40/1/80/1

LNWR 'Claughton' 4-6-0: 5902/33/5/63/83/92/7

LMS 'Patriot' 4-6-0: 6001/11/2/25, 5968/84

LMS Class '7F' 0-8-0: 9537-40

LMS 'Crab' 2-6-0: 13052/3, 13131-5

Farnley Junction (1934 Allocation)

LYR Class '4P' 4-6-0: 5793/4/6-5801/3

LNWR Class '4P' 4-6-0: 8724/5/7/56-64

LNWR Class '7F' 0-8-0: 8893-5, 8964/6, 9013/8/52-5, 9106/23, 9297, 9377-9/81-3/5-7/9-94

LYR 'Dreadnought' 4-6-0: 10455/7/72-4

LYR Aspinall Class '2P' 2-4-2T: 10649/67, 10775, 10829/53/71

LYR Class '3F' 0-6-0: 12103/41/83, 12255/89

LMS 'Crab' 2-6-0: 13121/413

LMS Class 3F 0-6-0T: 16650/1/3-8

Copley Hill

Robinson Class 'B4' 4-6-0: 6096-6102

Ivatt Class 'C1' 4-4-2: 3280, 4423/33/53

Ivatt Class 'C12' 4-4-2T: 4010/4, 4501/31/2/5/8/40

Ivatt Class 'D3' 4-4-0: 4076

Robinson Class 'D10' 4-4-0: 5432/4

Stirling Class 'J2' 0-6-0: 3079

Stirling Class 'J3' 0-6-0: 4110/32/72

Gresley Class 'J50' 0-6-0T: 593/4, 3214/38

Ivatt Class 'J52' 0-6-0ST: 3963

Gresley Class 'K3' 2-6-0: 202/3

Ivatt Class 'N1' 0-6-2T: 4556/60/6/92

Neville Hill

Raven Class 'A7' 4-6-2T: 1180/3/5/95

Raven Class 'B13' 4-6-0: 753/62

Raven Class 'B15' 4-6-0: 819/24

Raven Class 'B16' 4-6-0: 1380/83

Worsdell Class 'D17' 4-4-0: 1877, 1903/5/8/23

Worsdell Class 'D20' 4-4-0: 2011, 2018

Worsdell Class 'D21' 4-4-0: 1237-40/3-6

Gresley Class 'D49' 4-4-0: 201/11/20/34/6/45/51/73/82

Worsdell Class 'F5' 2-4-2T: 1579

Worsdell Class 'G5' 0-4-4T: 580, 1096, 1883, 1911

Raven Class 'H1' 4-4-4T: 1326, 1518/20, 2143/7/61

Worsdell Class 'J21' 0-6-0: 300, 619, 806, 1515/67/9, 1805/6/14

Worsdell Class 'J25' 0-6-0: 1970/7, 2034/67

Raven Class 'J27' 0-6-0: 1213

Gresley Class 'J39' 0-6-0: 1453/69

Worsdell Class 'J71' 0-6-0T: 811, 1835

Worsdell Class 'J72' 0-6-0T: 512/6

Raven Class 'J77' 0-6-0T: 1460/2

Worsdell Class 'N8' 0-6-2T: 213

Worsdell Class 'N10' 0-6-2T: 1132, 1317

Worsdell Class 'Q5' 0-8-0: 430

Raven Class 'Q6' 0-8-0: 2282, 2298

Right:
No 1 bay platform at Exchange station. *LYRS*

Appendix 2
Allocation of Locomotives, 1955

Holbeck (20A)

Stanier Class '3' 2-6-2T: 40148, 40169, 40193

Fowler (rebuilt) Class '2P' 4-4-0: 40323, 40518

Compound Class '4P' 4-4-0: 41068, 41100, 41104, 41137

Ivatt Class '2' 2-6-2T: 41267

Hughes Class '6P5F' 2-6-0: 42771, 42774, 42795, 42798

Ivatt Class '4' 2-6-0: 43116, 43117

Fowler Class '4F' 0-6-0: 43858

LMS Class '4F' 0-6-0: 44055, 44207, 44501, 44582

Stanier Class '5' 4-6-0: 44662, 44753-57, 44826, 44828, 44849, 44852, 44853, 44854, 44857, 44943, 44983

Stanier 'Jubilee' 4-6-0: 45562 *Alberta*, 45564 *New South Wales*, 45565 *Victoria*, 45566 *Queensland*, 45568 *Western Australia*, 45569 *Tasmania*, 45573 *Newfoundland*, 45589 *Gwalior*, 45597 *Barbados*, 45605 *Cyprus*, 45608 *Gibraltar*, 45619 *Nigeria*, 45639 *Raleigh*, 45658 *Keyes*, 45659 *Drake*, 45675 *Hardy*, 45694 *Bellerophon*, 45739 *Ulster*

Stanier 'Royal Scot' 4-6-0: 46103 *Royal Scots Fusilier*, 46108 *Seaforth Highlander*, 46109 *Royal Engineer*, 46112 *Sherwood Forester*, 46113 *Cameronian*, 46117 *Welsh Guardsman*, 46133 *The Green Howards*, 46145 *The Duke of Wellington's Regt (West Riding)*

Ivatt Class '2' 2-6-0: 46453, 46493, 46497, 46498

Johnson Class '3F' 0-6-0T: 47254

LMS Class '3F' 0-6-0T: 47418, 47420, 47436

Stanier Class '8F' 2-8-0: 48067, 48104, 48157, 48158, 48159, 48283, 48396, 48399, 48537

BR Standard Class '5' 4-6-0: 73045, 73053, 73054, 73066

Stourton (20B)

Johnson Class '1F' 0-6-0T: 41797, 41838, 41859

Ivatt Class '4' 2-6-0: 43044

Johnson Class '3F' 0-6-0: 43392, 43456, 43579, 43586, 43681, 43737

Fowler Class '4F' 0-6-0: 43851, 43871, 43931, 43987

LMS Class '4F' 0-6-0: 44094, 44153, 44335, 44467, 44562, 44584, 44586

Johnson Class '3F' 0-6-0T: 47249

LMS Class '3F' 0-6-0T: 47271, 47463, 47538, 47589, 47632, 47640

Stanier Class '8F' 2-8-0: 48005, 48126, 48276, 48311, 48641, 48652, 48721

Farnley Junction (25G)

LMS Class '2P' 4-4-0: 40581, 40584, 40690

LMS Compound '4P' 4-4-0: 41101

Ivatt Class '2' 2-6-2T: 41254, 41255, 41256, 41257, 41258, 41259

Hughes Class '6P5F' 2-6-0: 42700, 42712

Stanier Class '5' 4-6-0: 44896, 45063, 45075, 45076, 45079, 45080, 45204, 45211, 45341

Stanier 'Jubilee' 4-6-0: 45581 *Bihar and Orissa*, 45646 *Napier*, 45695 *Minotaur*, 45705 *Seahorse*, 45708 *Resolution*

LMS Class '3F' 0-6-0T: 47567, 47568, 47569, 47570, 47571

Riddles 'Austerity' Class '8F' 2-8-0: 90308, 90322, 90336, 90351, 90372, 90395, 90407, 90527, 90562, 90588, 90591, 90645, 90649, 90650, 90664, 90666, 90684, 90698, 90699, 90711, 90726, 90728

Copley Hill (37B)

Gresley Class 'A3' 4-6-2: 60051 *Blink Bonny*,

60053 *Sansovino,* 60058 *Blair Athol,* 60106 *Flying Fox*

Peppercorn Class 'A1' 4-6-2: 60117 *Bois Roussel,* 60118 *Archibald Sturrock,* 60119 *Patrick Stirling,* 60120 *Kittiwake,* 60122 *Curlew,* 60131 *Osprey,* 60133 *Pommern,* 60134 *Foxhunter,* 60139 *Sea Eagle,* 60141 *Abbotsford*

Gresley Class 'V2' 2-6-2: 60859, 60865, 60913

Thompson Class 'B1' 4-6-0: 61129, 61309, 61386, 61387, 61388

Gresley Class 'J6' 0-6-0: 64173, 64276, 64277

Gresley Class 'J39' 0-6-0: 64911

Robinson Class 'C13' 4-4-2T: 67438

Gresley Class 'J50' 0-6-0T: 68911, 68913, 68925, 68978, 68984, 68988

Ivatt Class 'N1' 0-6-2T: 69430, 69444, 69450

Gresley Class 'N7' 0-6-2T: 69691, 69694, 69695, 69696

Neville Hill (508)

Gresley Class 'A3' 4-6-2: 60036 *Colombo,* 60074 *Harvester,* 60081 *Shotover,* 60084 *Trigo,* 60086 *Gainsborough*

Thompson Class 'B1' 4-6-0: 61017 *Bushbuck,* 61035 *Pronghorn,* 61062, 61065, 61069, 61086, 61216, 61218, 61237, 61240 *Harry Hinchcliffe,* 61256, 61257, 61259

Class 'B16' 4-6-0: 61410, 61411, 61412, 61413, 61414, 61415, 61425, 61427, 61428, 61429, 61431, 61432, 61433, 61440, 61442, 61446, 61447, 61469, 61470, 61471

Gresley Class 'D49' 4-4-0: 62742 *The Braes of Derwent,* 62748 *The Southwold,* 62764 *The Garth,* 62775 *The Tynedale*

Raven Class 'Q6' 0-8-0: 63348, 63436

Gresley Class 'J39' 0-6-0: 64758, 64791, 64835, 64860, 64863, 64920, 64933, 64934, 64935, 64943

Worsdell Class 'J25' 0-6-0: 65650, 65654

Worsdell Class 'G5' 0-4-4T: 67262, 67266, 67274, 67290

Worsdell Class 'J77' 0-6-0T: 68395

Worsdell Class 'J72' 0-6-0T: 68672, 68681

Worsdell Class 'N10' 0-6-2T: 69098

Sterling (H&BR) Class 'N13' 0-6-2T: 69114, 69117, 69119

Gresley Class 'A8' 4-6-2T: 69858, 69862

Bowling (Hammerton Street) (37C)

Thompson Class 'B1' 4-6-0: 61031 *Reedbuck,* 61229, 61230, 61267, 61268, 61296

Gresley Class 'O4' 2-8-0: 63920

Gresley Class 'J6' 0-6-0: 64170, 64203, 64226, 64268

Gresley Class 'J39' 0-6-0: 64903, 64907

Gresley Class 'J50' 0-6-0T: 68892, 68895, 68897, 68898, 68908, 68912, 68922, 68923, 68932, 68933, 68934, 68940, 68942, 68943, 68944, 68959, 68969

Ivatt Class 'N1' 0-6-2T: 69434, 69436, 69439, 69443, 69447, 69451, 69464, 69467, 69471, 69474, 69478

Low Moor (25F)

Ivatt Class '2' 2-6-2T: 41262, 41263, 41264

Fairburn/Stanier Class '4' 2-6-4T: 42107, 42108, 42109, 42188, 42189, 42649, 42650

Stanier Class '5' 4-6-0: 44693, 44694, 44695, 44912, 44946, 44951, 45207, 45208, 45210, 45219

Aspinall Class '2P' 2-4-2T: 50757, 50764, 50869

Aspinall Class '2F' 0-6-0ST: 51404

Aspinall Class '3F' 0-6-0: 52120, 52166, 52235, 52343, 52355, 52515, 52521

Manningham (20E)

Stanier Class '3' 2-6-2T: 40074, 40090, 40112, 40114, 40117, 40147, 40155, 40178

Fowler Class '2P' 4-4-0: 40562

LMS Compound '4P' 4-4-0: 41061, 41063

Ivatt Class '2' 2-6-2T: 41247, 41265, 41266

Fairburn/Fowler Class '4' 2-6-4T: 42051, 42052, 42138, 42139, 42380

Johnson Class '3F' 0-6-0: 43686, 43742, 43770

Fowler Class '3F' 0-6-0: 43784

Fowler Class '4F' 0-6-0: 43944

LMS Class '4F' 0-6-0: 44216, 44400

Johnson Class '3F' 0-6-0T: 47222, 47255

LMS Class '3F' 0-6-0T: 4741

Aspinall Class '2P' 2-4-2T: 50636, 50686, 50795

Appendix 3
Allocation of Locomotives, 1967

Holbeck (55A)

Fairburn/Stanier Class '4' 2-6-4T: 42145, 42622, 42609

Ivatt Class '4' 2-6-0: 43130

Stanier Class '5' 4-6-0: 44662, 44824, 44826, 44852, 44853, 44854, 44857, 44896, 44912, 44943, 44983, 45075, 45079, 45204, 45219, 45273

Stanier 'Jubilee' 4-6-0: 45562 *Alberta*, 45593 *Kolhapur*, 45647 *Sturdee*, 45675 *Hardy*, 45697 *Achilles*

Stanier Class '8F' 2-8-0: 48104, 48157, 48158, 48283, 48399, 48454, 48542

Stourton (55B)

Ivatt Class '4' 2-6-0: 43084, 43140

Stanier Class '5' 4-6-0: 45080, 45211, 45458

Stanier Class '8F' 2-8-0: 48084, 48093, 48126, 48130, 48622, 48703

Manningham (55F)

Fairburn Class '4' 2-6-4T: 42052, 42072, 42085, 42093, 42138, 42152, 42189

Ivatt Class '4' 2-6-0: 43044, 43050, 43081, 43096, 43117

Low Moor (56F)

Fairburn Class '4' 2-6-4T: 42055, 42073, 42116, 42196, 42233, 42235

Stanier Class '5' 4-6-0: 44693, 44694, 44695, 45208

Stanier 'Jubilee' 4-6-0: 45565 *Victoria*

Riddles 'Austerity' '8F' 2-8-0: 90711

Below:
Queensbury station where the former Bradford-Keighley platform viaduct still stands, but is partly obscured by infill tipping. *S. R. Batty*

Appendix 4
List of Railway Company Abbreviations

BR	British Railways	**LBHJR**	Leeds, Bradford & Halifax Junction Railway
B&T	Bradford & Thornton Railway	**LD&HR**	Leeds, Dewsbury & Huddersfield Railway
BE&IR	Bradford, Eccleshill & Idle Railway	**LD&MR**	Leeds, Dewsbury & Manchester Railway
BTC	British Transport Commission	**L&MR**	Liverpool & Manchester Railway
BW&LR	Bradford, Wakefield & Leeds Railway	**LMSR**	London, Midland & Scottish Railway
ELR	East Lancashire Railway	**LNWR**	London & North Western Railway
GCR	Great Central Railway	**L&S**	Leeds & Selby Railway
GER	Great Eastern Railway	**L&TR**	Leeds & Thirsk Railway
GNR	Great Northern Railway	**L&WRJ**	Leeds & West Riding Junction Railway
GWR	Great Western Railway	**LYR**	Lancashire & Yorkshire Railway
HBR	Hull & Barnsley Railway	**L&YR**	London & York Railway
H&MR	Huddersfield & Manchester Railway	**MSLR**	Manchester, Sheffield & Lincolnshire Railway
H&SJR	Huddersfield & Sheffield Junction Railway	**M&LR**	Manchester & Leeds Railway
H&SR	Hull & Selby Railway	**NBR**	North British Railway
I&SR	Idle & Shipley Railway	**NER**	North Eastern Railway
KWVR	Keighley & Worth Valley Railway	**NMR**	North Midland Railway
L&BR	Leeds & Bradford Railway	**T&KR**	Thornton & Keighley Railway
		WP&GR	Wakefield, Pontefract & Goole Railway
		WRG	West Riding & Grimsby Railway
		WRUR	West Riding Union Railway
		WYR	West Yorkshire Railway
		Y&NMR	York & North Midland Railway

Below:
'Highflyer' Atlantic No 1406 at Low Moor shed in early LMS days, with LNWR-style livery. *LYRS*

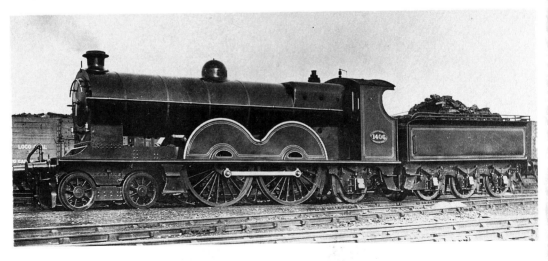

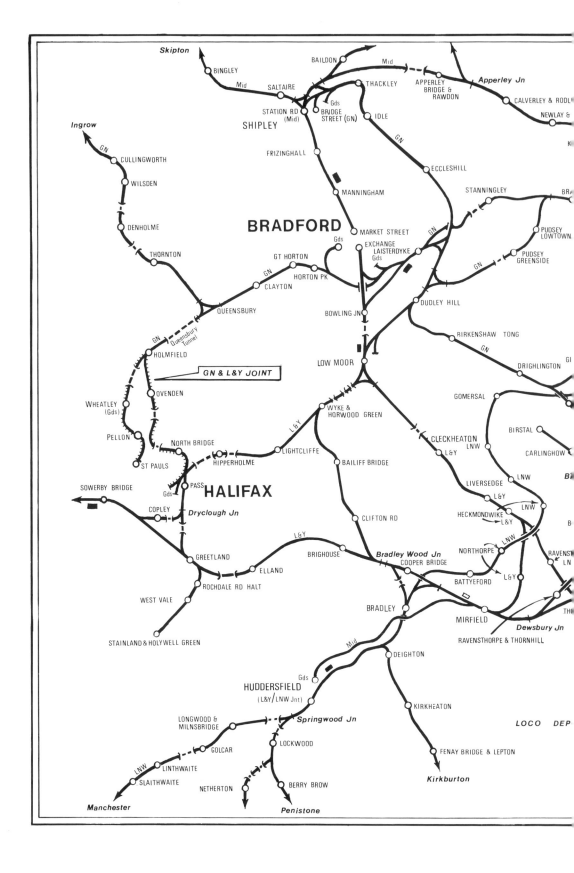